Thinking Together

By the same author:

Thinking Stories 1: Philosophical Inquiry for Children
Thinking Stories 1: Teacher Resource/Activity Book
Thinking Stories 2: Philosophical Inquiry for Children
Thinking Stories 2: Teacher Resource/Activity Book

Thinking Together

Philosophical Inquiry for the Classroom

Philip Cam

PRIMARY ENGLISH TEACHING ASSOCIATION
AND
Hale & Iremonger

For Heather

First edition
10 9 8 7 6 5 4 3 2 1

Typeset by
Southwood Press Pty Limited
80–92 Chapel Street, Marrickville, NSW

Printed & bound by
Australian Print Group
Maryborough, Victoria

For the publisher
Hale & Iremonger Pty Limited
GPO Box 2552, Sydney, NSW

National Library of Australia Cataloguing-in-publication entry

Cam, Philip, 1948-

   Thinking together: philosophical inquiry for the classroom.

   Bibliography.
   ISBN 0 86806 508 0 (pbk).

   1. Philosophy – Study and teaching (Primary). 2. Children's stories – Study and teaching (Primary). I. Primary English Teaching Association (Australia). II. Title.

372.8

Photographs on pages 10, 17, 37 and 38:
Courtesy of Martyn Mather, Paddington Public School

Cover by
Ken Rinkel
One Plus One Design Pty Ltd
PO Box 157, Narrabeen NSW

Contents

Introduction

'It would be wonderful to introduce classes in thinking to our school, but the timetable is so crowded.' This familiar lament strikes me as odd. It's as if the teaching of thinking were an addition to the curriculum, like a class in drama or the inclusion of a language other than English. Yet teaching children to think – whatever that might mean – can't be yet another subject area to be fitted into the curriculum. What would you say if a colleague suggested that perhaps a little thinking could be squeezed in on Wednesdays before lunch? Wouldn't it seem like an attempt at somewhat cynical humour?

As these remarks suggest, thinking is not a special subject or activity in addition to others, but has to do with the way we approach a topic or subject or engage in an activity. It applies to all areas of the existing curriculum. We want children to approach all their learning in a way that is productive and intelligent. We don't want to see unproductive or unintelligent behaviour in our students. We don't want to see thoughtless or inconsiderate behaviour either, for that matter. The two sets of things are related.

Having said this, I'm about to advocate the introduction of philosophy as a means of placing thinking firmly at the centre of a primary education, and that may well look like an addition to the timetable. It may also look like a misconception, since it suggests that thinking might indeed have its own slot in the school day. I admit that there's some truth to these perceptions, but let's consider the matter further.

Philosophy is unlike other subjects in two important respects. First, although the fact is much neglected in our educational system, philosophical questions and issues can take us to the very heart of other subjects. They make us *really think* about their subject matter. Secondly, philosophy is specifically concerned with *good thinking*. Its procedures are effective intellectual operations and its tools are a means to that end.

As I hope to make clear in *Thinking Together*, these two features place philosophy in a unique position to help children become more effective thinkers. In addition, what I advocate is not the inclusion of philosophy as a *subject area* so much as an *approach* to what teachers already do in existing teaching areas. Philosophical inquiry is something that you can build into your literacy program, into personal development, social sciences, science and technology, and so on.

It's a central theme of this book that we can most profitably nurture good thinking in the classroom by encouraging children to inquire and reason together about things of significance. For one thing, much of the thinking that we do in our lives involves us in reasoning with others – with members of our family, our friends, and those with whom we work. For another, as I will explain, it is largely through the internalisation of social practices that the individual's habits of thought are formed. This gives us all the more reason to establish good social practices in the formative years.

Accordingly, the main learning experience I am concerned with is classroom discussion, where attention is paid to the skills and dispositions of thinking together – to such basic things as asking questions, giving reasons, sticking to the point, being fair-minded, listening to alternative points of view and exploring disagreement. Attention is also paid to children's conceptual development and fostering a deeper understanding of issues and ideas. I offer a good deal of practical advice to the teacher about guiding this kind of investigation, and show how it can be used to develop children's thinking skills and dispositions, while enriching their concepts and deepening their understandings.

The other main focus of *Thinking Together* is the use of narrative. While the teacher will be able to find many other means of stimulating children's philosophical imaginations, children's literature is a particularly rich source of philosophical themes. By selecting appropriate story materials for class discussion, the teacher will be able to provide children with an effective stimulus for philosophical inquiry into many different topics over a wide variety of subject areas. Children's responses can then be used to initiate conceptual exploration and reasoning, and that search for meaning which is central to philosophy. I discuss the use of stories throughout the book, and I have included two chapters that deal specifically with selecting story materials and planning discussion around them.

Over recent years I have had the great pleasure of exploring these ideas with teachers and children both in Australia and overseas, and of coming to understand some of their possibilities by devising curriculum materials for the primary school. All the same, I can claim little credit for the principles and practices recommended in this book, which owe so much to others. The pioneering work of Matthew Lipman and Ann Margaret Sharp must be particularly acknowledged, and I am also mindful of those, too numerous to mention, who by good fortune I have come to know in the truly international community that they have inspired. I would also like to express my gratitude to Jeremy Steele, Vivienne Nicoll-Hatton and the other members of the PETA Publications Committee who offered valuable comments on the manuscript.

PART I

An Invitation to Inquiry

CHAPTER ONE

Learning to Think

It is fortunate that once we know how to do most things, we can do them without thinking about them. Consider walking, talking, or riding a bicycle. If you had to think about how to walk when you wanted to move about, or how to talk whenever you wanted to say something, then it might be said that you hardly know how to do these things, or at least that you're not fully proficient. If you have to think about how to ride a bicycle when you get on one, then either you're just learning or else you've all but forgotten how to do it.

Many of the skills that are taught and the understandings that are acquired in lower, middle and upper primary school are like those of the cyclist in that eventually they become automatic, or nearly so; and in many respects, the more automatic the execution becomes the better the child's performance. We may call these skills and understandings *routine*. As children learn to read fluently, spell reliably or multiply easily, for example, they move along that road.

There are other accomplishments which are just the reverse. These are the things that we do well only once we have learned to *think* when we do them. They are those practices which are *reflective*. People who can spell difficult words without having to think much about it are proficient spellers, whereas people who habitually act without thinking of the consequences of their actions are not proficient in action. Their behaviour tends to be rash, thoughtless or inconsiderate, and they have a lot to learn about wise conduct. Similarly, people who seldom consider more than one possibility, or tend to reject alternative courses of action without weighing their merits, show themselves to be unimaginative, dogmatic or inflexible thinkers, who haven't learned how to make the best of their opportunities.

Skills and practices of both kinds must be developed in the classroom. Children who have learned to speak fluently but whose speech is thoughtless or inconsiderate are likely to hurt themselves and others. A child who has memorised lots of facts but doesn't know how to explore possibilities will not be able to put that knowledge to very much use. The message here is that unless we pay attention to skills and practices of both kinds – *the routine and the reflective* – we will fail to educate children to be truly intelligent in their thought and reasonable in their action.

Thinking of the reflective kind is a necessary complement to the so-called basics of education, and this book explores one way of helping children to develop it. Before we begin that exploration, however, I will say a little more about the kind of thinking that I have in mind, and then introduce some ideas that underlie the subsequent discussion.

Beyond Routine Thinking

The term 'reflective thinking' comes from John Dewey. As Dewey defines it, reflective thinking is the

> active, persistent, and careful consideration of any belief or supposed form of knowledge in the light of the grounds that support it, and the further conclusions to which it tends . . . it is a conscious and voluntary effort to establish belief upon a firm basis of reasons.[1]

What Dewey describes here is a persistent act of inquiry, where there is order to our thought, and it builds in one way or another toward considered judgement. As Dewey goes on to argue, reflective thinking doesn't occur by 'spontaneous combustion'. It occurs when we feel the need of a resolution because we are doubtful, puzzled or perplexed. It is because there is some problem or difficulty to overcome that our thoughts are so directed. On Dewey's conception, then, reflective thinking is a process by which we examine the grounds and consequences of our beliefs in order to solve a problem that has unsettled us to some degree or other.

The stimulus for reflective thinking is familiar outside the classroom. In many areas of our lives we encounter problems, strike obstacles or face dilemmas; questions can trouble us, and the meaning of circumstances and events is sometimes ambiguous or indistinct. In these kinds of circumstances it's quite normal to feel puzzled and uncertain, even confused or perplexed. It is here that reflective thinking is most likely to take hold. We need a plan, some explanation, or a resolution of some kind. So we begin to look for likely reasons or possible causes.

We marshal our facts and look for further evidence or fresh clues. We canvas others for suggestions. We begin to think about the implications of various courses of action. And we hold fire, if we are wise, until we have completed our reconnoitre and drawn up some plan of attack.

Obviously we don't want to disturb, confuse or perplex children in the class-room. Yet we do need to provoke puzzlement, stimulate curiosity and rely upon the children's sense of wonder. This was vitally important for Dewey, who held that learning to think well should be regarded as the fundamental aim of an elementary education. It is no less important if we regard reflective thinking as the woof that transforms the warp of routine thinking into the whole cloth of effective thought.

The influence of Dewey's conception of reflective thinking can be seen in the many texts over the years whose chapters and titles bear that name.[2] It can also be found in more recent conceptions of thinking, such as that offered by Robert Ennis, a prominent figure in the critical thinking movement, who defines critical thinking as 'reasonable reflective thinking that is focused on deciding what to believe or do'.[3]

Having made this tie between reflective and critical thinking, it is important to say something about their relation to *creative thinking*. Ennis makes the point that, on his definition, critical thinking does not exclude creative thinking. He says: 'Formulating hypotheses, alternative ways of viewing a problem, questions, possible solutions, and plans for investigating something are creative acts that come under this definition.'[4] Ennis is right to say that he hasn't *excluded* creative thinking, and by extension, the same would apply to Dewey. Yet in both cases their emphasis is more on the critical rather than the creative side. Certainly Dewey distinguishes between reflective thinking and thinking which, however similar, has an essentially aesthetic, affective or imaginative basis:

> The imaginative stories poured forth by children possess all degrees of internal congruity; some are disjointed, some are articulated. When connected, they simulate reflective thought; indeed, they usually occur in minds of logical capacity. These imaginative enterprises often precede thinking of the close-knit type and prepare the way for it. But *they do not aim at knowledge, at belief about the facts or in truths*; and thereby they are marked off from reflective thought even when they most resemble it. Those who express such thoughts do not expect credence, but rather credit for a well-constructed plot or a well-arranged climax. They produce good stories, not – unless by chance – knowledge.[5]

When Dewey contrasts thought that aims at 'belief about the facts' with 'imaginative enterprises' that aim at such things as narrative integrity, he appears to exclude a great deal of creative thinking from the category of reflective thinking. Thereby he fails to include much of the non-routine thinking that we want to encourage in the classroom. He seems to exclude a great deal of philosophical thought as well. So although Dewey's idea of reflective thinking captures much of what we want, it is ultimately too narrow for our purposes.

This is where the philosopher and educationalist Matthew Lipman has come to our aid. A thinker whose concern with reflective education is deeply influenced by Dewey, Lipman argues that excellent thinking is at once critical, creative, and complex.[6]

Thinking which is both critical and creative, says Lipman, aims not just at justified belief or literal truth, but at the refashioning and creation of meaning – at imagining possibilities, developing concepts, and enlarging ideas in many directions. Excellent thinking may be consumed more by one of these ends than the other, but it will be regulated by both of them. In fact, no matter how exclusively critical our thought, critical thinking will always be a little creative, just as all creative thinking will be at least somewhat critical. So in fact, both critical and creative thinking are aspects or tendencies of all non-routine thinking, which Lipman calls *higher-order thinking*.[7]

As Lipman goes on to remind us, excellent thinking not only brings a critical and creative approach to its subject matter, it also pays attention to its own procedures. To use Lipman's term, excellent thinking is *complex thinking* in that it is thinking which is self-conscious. In being aware of its own way of going about things, its own method or approach, complex thinking is sensitive to its own limitations and possibilities. It is not like a cook who is totally absorbed in the recipe. Neither is it like the card player who's continually moving out of turn. It pays attention to both the substance and its procedures as it moves along.

Lipman's main interest is in how best to promote critical, creative and complex thinking in the classroom. His view is that the richest resource at our disposal is philosophy. It is the addition of philosophy, more than anything else, that can help to make adequate provision for thinking in the classroom. At first this might seem like an odd proposal. We tend to associate philosophy with the university lecture hall rather than the primary classroom. For some people, the word 'philosophy' conjures up an almost unintelligible ivory tower discipline most suitable for the bookish adult. Yet no one who is familiar with Lipman's stories for children, or who has seen children engaged in philosophical inquiry in any number of classrooms around the country, would confuse this stereotype of academic philosophy with philosophy for children.

While people need to judge these things at first hand, the main undertaking in *Thinking Together* is to explore how we can begin to put Lipman's proposal into effect. In the next chapter I will begin this exploration by considering the questions, tools and procedures of philosophical inquiry from an educational perspective. But first we need to consider one more aspect of thinking which informs the book: the importance of learning to think by thinking together.

Why Thinking *Together?*

According to the Russian psychologist Lev Vygotsky, although thought and talk have different roots, they converge in early childhood.[8] Well before children are of school age, they can use speech not only for social or communicative purposes, but also to communicate with themselves in solving problems and organising their own behaviour. And this speech for oneself – egocentric speech, as it's called – will be the seed of cultivated thought.

Through egocentric speech children address themselves in the ways they have previously learned to address others, and this marks a change in their psychological orientation. They begin to attend to their own thinking. Consequently, children begin to gain control over their thoughts, and they start to become more self-directed in their behaviour. They become less impulsive and more able to overcome problems by planning.

According to Vygotsky, egocentric speech gradually makes its way inward – it becomes inner speech – and by this means a socialised intellect is able to develop:

> The greatest change in children's capacity to use language as a problem-solving tool takes place . . . when socialised speech (which has previously been used to address an adult) *is turned inward*. Instead of appealing to the adult, children appeal to themselves; language thus takes on an *intrapersonal function* in addition to its *interpersonal use*. When children develop a method of behaviour for guiding themselves that had previously been used in relation to another person, when they organise their own activities according to a social form of behaviour, they succeed in applying the social attitude to themselves. The history of the internalisation of social speech is also the history of the socialisation of children's practical intellect.[9]

On Vygotsky's account, this incorporation and transformation of the social is a universal feature in the development of the so-called higher cognitive functions:

> Every function in the child's cultural development appears twice: first on the social level, and later, on the individual level; first *between* people (*interpsychological*), and then *inside* the child (*intrapsychological*). This applies equally to voluntary attention, to logical memory, and to the formation of concepts. All the higher psychological functions originate as actual relations between human individuals.[10]

When we think about developing a child's capacities to think in the classroom, therefore, it would be a natural extension of Vygotsky's remarks to suggest that the basic features of critical and creative thought may become internalised in much the same way: that children who engage in *social practices* which are critical and creative come to internalise them; and that by paying attention to the processes involved in *thinking together*, children will come to pay attention to the processes involved in their own thinking.

Through thinking together, children learn to pay attention to the processes
of their own thinking

It may be that we come to think for ourselves by assimilating our teachers and critics. The philosopher Gilbert Ryle once suggested that when we think in the sense that Rodin's *Le Penseur* is supposed to be thinking, we attempt to make headway by trying out on ourselves 'expedients, routines, procedures, exercises, curbs, and dodges of types which teachers do employ, not always successfully, when they want to teach things that they know to pupils who do not'.[11] We internalise the teacher, in effect, adopting the teacher's role while remaining the pupil and exercising the teacher's strategies upon ourselves from within.

These themes are also to be found in the writings of the philosopher-psychologist George Herbert Mead.[12] According to Mead, human beings would never have developed self-awareness or become selves without the capacity to talk to themselves. Even closer to Vygotsky, Mead says that the self develops through an internalisation of the forms of regard involved in our communion with others. From our early years, we begin to make ourselves the object of our own social attention. We offer ourselves encouragement, advice, and rather firmer instruction. We praise ourselves and blame ourselves. We inflict punishment upon ourselves and offer ourselves rewards. We come to address ourselves as we address others, and in so doing we become a self to ourselves.

Once again, in the classroom we can promote self-development by having children engage each other in the practice of reflective reason. Over time, the kinds of interpersonal regard embodied in the social practice of thinking together will be reflected inward. There they will help to nurture the *self*-regard from which reflective and reasonable selves will grow.

In summary, the development of thinking which is at once critical, creative and complex should be as much the aim of primary education as the development of thinking which is more routine. Since children develop intellectually by internalising social practices, the best way of fostering good thinking in the classroom is through the social and intellectual practice of thinking together. Given its special concern with good thinking, and its ability to make us think about a wide array of subject matter, philosophy can play a special role in this enterprise. By adapting it to these ends, philosophical inquiry can be a very effective means of promoting good thinking in the classroom.

In order to see how philosophical inquiry may function as an educational activity, we need to look at the nature of philosophical questions and at the kinds of tools and procedures that it employs. That is the topic of the next chapter.

NOTES

1. John Dewey, *How We Think* (New York: D.C. Heath, 1933), p. 6.
2. See for example, H. Gordon Hullfish and Philip G. Smith, *Reflective Thinking: The Method of Education* (New York: Dodd, Mead & Company, 1967), and L. Susan Stebbing, *A Modern Introduction to Logic* (London: Methuen, 1931), Chapter 1, 'Reflective Thinking in Ordinary Life'. See also the chapter from Lipman's *Thinking in Education* cited below.
3. Robert H. Ennis, 'A Taxonomy of Critical Thinking Dispositions and Abilities' in Joan Boykoff Baron & Robert J. Sternberg (eds), *Teaching Thinking Skills: Theory and Practice* (New York: W. H. Freeman, 1987), p. 10. Ennis has developed a detailed list of goals for a critical thinking curriculum, set out in terms of the skills and abilities implied by his definition of critical thinking. While this isn't the place to compare Ennis' list with that which could be drawn from Dewey, it is worth noting that, in Dewey's terms, Ennis' definition is somewhat redundant. For Dewey, reflective thinking just is reasonable thinking that is focused on what to do or believe. Matters of detail aside, therefore, critical thinking, as it's understood by Ennis, is Dewey's reflective thinking.
4. Ibid.
5. *How We Think*, pp. 3-4.
6. See Matthew Lipman, *Thinking in Education* (New York: Cambridge University Press, 1991), Chapter 1, 'The reflective model of educational practice'.
7. This at once confirms Ennis' claim that a concentration on critical thinking doesn't exclude creative thinking, while making it clear that the kind of thinking he wishes to promote is guided more by the star of truth than that of meaning. The idea of higher-order thinking may be somewhat vague, as Ennis complains, but it enables us to see why a heavy emphasis on critical thinking gives us only one end of the range.

8. See Lev S. Vygotsky, *Thought and Language* (Cambridge, Mass: MIT Press, 1962), especially Chapter 4, 'The genetic roots of thought and speech'.
9. L. S. Vygotsky, *Mind in Society: The Development of Higher Psychological Processes*, edited by Michael Cole, Vera John-Steiner, Sylvia Scribner and Ellen Souberman (Cambridge, Mass: Harvard University Press, 1978), p. 27.
10. Ibid., p. 57.
11. Gilbert Ryle, 'Thinking and self-teaching,' *Rice University Studies*, Vol. 58, No. 3 (1972). Reproduced in Matthew Lipman, *Thinking Children and Education* (Dubuque, Iowa: Kendall/Hunt, 1993).
12. George Herbert Mead, *Mind, Self, and Society* (Chicago: University of Chicago Press, 1934). See also A. Reck (ed.), *Selected Writings of George Herbert Mead* (Chicago: University of Chicago Press, 1964) and Bernard N. Meltzer, 'Mead's Social Psychology' in John Pickering and Martin Skinner (eds), *From Sentience to Symbols: Readings in Consciousness* (Harvester Wheatsheaf, 1990).

CHAPTER TWO

Philosophical Inquiry as an Educational Activity

Although philosophy has not traditionally been thought of as a suitable subject for children, Matthew Lipman has argued that children can engage in genuine philosophical inquiry provided that it is reconstructed in ways that suit their talents and their interests.[1] Over the past twenty-five years he has written a series of extended narratives for children, which draw upon a rich array of philosophical themes taken from the history of philosophy.[2] In Lipman's novels, we find children discovering philosophy for themselves as they try to make sense of their experience and deal with the problems that confront them in daily life. We see them thinking together as they acquire the tools and learn the procedures of philosophical inquiry that are built into the narrative. In short, we see the problems and issues that philosophers have discussed falling into the hands of children, who come to philosophy like ducks to water.

These narratives, together with the extensive teacher support materials that Lipman and his associates have produced, present a model of what children's philosophy might be like, of how it can be instituted in the classroom, and of how we can bring the philosophical content of the various learning areas to life. Yet I suspect it's not so much the philosophical content that has helped Lipman's ideas and his materials to find their way into schools all over the world, but the connection of philosophy with thinking and enhanced learning. What appeals to educators more than anything else is the discovery that the wide-ranging content of philosophy and the nature of its methods make it a natural choice for promoting thinking in many areas of the school curriculum, and an invaluable means of helping children to become more effective participants in the learning process.

In order to see why philosophy offers such rich rewards, we need to know a little about the nature of its questions, its tools and procedures. So I am going to say just a little about them now. Once I have done that, it will be much easier to appreciate how philosophical inquiry can be adapted to the classroom. In subsequent chapters I will expand upon these brief remarks in considerable detail.

Philosophical Questions

Although often neglected or unacknowledged, philosophical questions pertain to all areas of the curriculum. Academic philosophy itself reflects this fact in the various specialist areas it contains, such as philosophy of science, aesthetics, social and political philosophy, philosophy and literature, philosophy of mind, of biology, of law, and so on. Many philosophical questions also have a wide scope, reflecting the concerns of a range of disciplines. In the context of school education, you can get some idea of the underlying philosophical content of the disciplines and the wide-ranging nature of many philosophical questions by taking a sample of these questions and listing the learning areas with which they are connected. For example:

PHILOSOPHICAL QUESTION	LEARNING AREAS
• What is it to be a person?	Personal development, social studies, literature
• What is a rule?	Social studies, mathematics, language, music, personal development, sport
• What makes something beautiful?	Art, music, literature, science and environmental education, mathematics
• What is a work of art?	Art, music, literature
• What is meaning?	Language and literature, music, art, mathematics
• Does everything have a cause?	Science education, social studies
• Do we have a responsibility for nature?	Science and environmental education, social studies
• What makes an action wrong?	Social studies, personal development, literature
• What is it to explain something?	Science, social studies, mathematics
• What is knowledge and how can we come by it?	All curriculum areas

Such broad interdisciplinary questions contrast sharply with those that once predominated in the classroom. In contrast to questions which call upon children to show their knowledge of established facts, or to apply rules for computation, to give a spelling and so on, philosophical questions are essentially contentious. They don't call for the correct answer. They demand further investigation and admit of different answers that may have one merit or another. They point to problems that cannot be solved by calculation, or by consulting a book, or by remembering what the teacher has said. *They require children to think for themselves.*

Naturally routine questions have an important role to play in the classroom. But fortunately, over recent years, we have come to understand the importance of also employing more open-ended questions that invite reflection. The claim here is that philosophical questions are a paradigm of the latter kind of question.

Considering the nature of its questions, philosophy should not be thought of as the isolated, esoteric discipline it is commonly taken to be, but as one that makes connections between and supports understanding in other disciplines. We might think of it as a Grand Central Station from which branch lines lead out to other disciplines, and through which we can travel backwards and forwards in many directions. To vary the metaphor, rather than regarding philosophy as an eccentric addition to primary education, we would do better to think of it as a hub for the educational wheel.

Philosophical Tools and Procedures

When surgeons perform operations, they select suitable instruments and use them to execute procedures that are known to be reliable. By analogy, when philosophers set to work on a problem, they reach for appropriate intellectual instruments and look to reliable ways of thinking. Because the philosopher's tools and procedures are aids and guides to thought, philosophy always has its eye on the thinking process. To use a recently fashionable term, it is a highly meta-cognitive discipline. It engages not only in thinking about philosophical topics, but also in quite a lot of reflection on its own thinking. This is one reason why it makes such a valuable educational resource. To the extent that primary education is a grounding in good thinking practices, philosophy, being very much in the business of good thinking, can provide it with strong support.

Children can learn to use many tools from the philosopher's kit. These include tools for such tasks as:

- exploring conceptual boundaries

- discovering criteria

- uncovering conceptual connections

- defining terms
- classifying objects
- identifying logical relations
- drawing deductive inferences
- analysing conditional statements
- constructing analogies.

By adapting these tools to the classroom and teaching children how to use them, we will be helping to build the kinds of mental habits that promote rich conceptual development and robust reasoning. We will also be developing the kinds of habits that make children more effective participants in their own intellectual development, and more able to think for themselves. In Chapters 6 and 7 we will be looking at some of the tools which can be used for these purposes.

Apart from specific instruments, there are general procedures for intellectual inquiry that we can adapt to the classroom. Even though philosophy can be a rather technical discipline, its basic procedures are not so very different from reflective thinking wherever it is found – whether in a primary classroom, in everyday life or a university tutorial. They include such things as:

- asking appropriate questions
- making useful distinctions
- drawing relevant inferences
- investigating questionable assumptions
- looking for significant consequences
- exploring possibilities
- seeking better alternatives
- giving and seeking reasons
- making considered judgements.

In adapting philosophy to the classroom, special attention is paid to these basic procedures. If you reflect upon it, you will realise that such procedures support good practice in any discipline, and that those who make it their habit to use them will bring an intelligent approach to whatever they do.

The Community of Inquiry

In order to realise the possibilities that philosophy has to offer, we need an appropriate framework for philosophical inquiry. Since the model of learning we are

The teacher's role is a complex and changing one. Here the teacher listens attentively to children who are engaged in a class discussion

following takes us from social practices and external acts to individual practices and mental acts, this will be an arrangement in which the children learn inquiry as a social practice and then internalise it. In other words, it will be one in which children learn to inquire together. It follows from the model that if we want children to question themselves, they should first learn to question one another. If they are to reason with themselves, they must first learn to reason with one another. If they are to think of how things stand from the other's point of view, they should first learn to inquire of the other. In sum, if we want children to learn how to think for themselves, we should engage them in thinking together.

Considering this, we are bound to treat the basic philosophical procedures we identified as first and foremost processes of intellectual exchange. The most obvious arrangement for such exchange is classroom discussion. It will be discussion in which children ask each other questions, give one another reasons, listen to each other's point of view, and so on for all the other procedures that we need to list. This is obviously a co-operative activity, in which the class becomes a community of people who are inquiring together – what Lipman calls a *community of inquiry*. Since the inquiry is a philosophical one, we can say that it's a philosophical community of inquiry.

The teacher's role in the community of inquiry is a complex and a changing one: here the teacher is a guide, there a conductor, and perhaps an ordinary contributor on some other occasion. Certainly, the teacher needs to guide the children in the ways of inquiry. If the children are to learn how to run their inquiry, they need to be taught. Yet the teacher must not be dominant or directive in ways that make it difficult for the children to take the reins. Knowing how and when to 'pass the reins' or to take them back is every bit as important as knowing your way around in inquiry. It demands considerable pedagogical skill. So if you feel a bit uncomfortable with your first efforts, don't worry. Once you and your students get the feel of it, the skills will rapidly build; and philosophical discussion can be a most enjoyable and rewarding affair even when things don't go quite as well as you all might wish. The practicalities of building a community of inquiry are discussed at length in Chapter 4, where you will find some detailed advice about conducting discussion.

Teaching Materials

Children will not engage in genuine philosophical inquiry unless the problem or issue under discussion *touches upon their interests, fires their imaginations, or otherwise moves them*. So teaching materials will not work unless they arouse philosophical interest. A text which merely told children about the nature of philosophy or explained philosophical ideas would be quite the wrong kind of thing. Apart from anything else, it would signal to children that philosophy is something they will learn about, rather than something they will do. On the other hand, narrative is a very powerful stimulus. It engages with children's emotions, attitudes and values, and appeals to their imaginations. Whether in the form of purpose-written stories, carefully selected children's literature, film or drama, narrative is a magnet for their interest and draws children in. It is just the thing that children need to get them thinking.

Whatever materials you use should have both philosophical potential and present matters in a way that opens them up for inquiry. Purpose-written materials will satisfy these demands, of course, because they were specifically designed that way. A broad array of children's literature and other kinds of stimulus material is also suitable, though you must work out what to use. That's not the difficult task that it might initially seem, as you will discover in Chapter 3, where we will look at the kinds of things you need to keep in mind when choosing reading material.

Finally, as you and your children begin to make your way in philosophical inquiry, you will find it useful to have a discussion plan. This helps to shape the discussion, where that is required, through a sequence of questions that explore a concept, problem or issue. In addition, there are exercises of many kinds that can extend the inquiry and complement discussion. Existing materials again offer the advantage of providing ready-made exercises and discussion plans, but regardless of whether you use and adapt them or devise your own, it is important to understand how they are meant to function. We come to this in Chapter 5, which deals with some basic principles for constructing discussion plans and takes you through sample exercises, so that you are familiar with these aids.

NOTES

1. See Matthew Lipman, Ann Margaret Sharp & Frederick S. Oscanyan, *Philosophy in the Classroom*, 2nd ed. (Philadelphia: Temple University Press, 1980); Matthew Lipman, *Philosophy Goes to School* (Philadelphia: Temple University Press, 1988); Matthew Lipman, *Thinking in Education* (New York: Cambridge University Press, 1991).
2. A list of Lipman's narratives for children can be found in the section, 'Children's Books and Classroom Materials', in the bibliography.

PART II

Tasks for the Teacher

CHAPTER THREE

Selecting Story Material

When it comes to selecting material for classroom inquiry, there are obviously criteria that you need to apply. I will discuss these criteria in a moment, and then I will take you through a story to show you the kinds of things to look for in identifying a narrative's philosophical content. However, in children's literature you are unlikely to find many stories that meet *all* of the criteria discussed. Instead, you will be looking for stories having the main features that I will describe, and apart from that you will simply need to exercise judgement as to whether various other features or the lack of them makes the material unsuitable. As you'll see, the story given at the end of this chapter is not ideal, even though it could be made to serve the purposes of classroom inquiry quite well.

Philosophical Themes

The first thing to look for in a story is whether it contains anything of philosophical promise. I will show you examples of such stories shortly, but let me assure you at the outset that you don't need an academic education in philosophy in order to make a well-informed decision. Simply ask yourself whether the story raises – or even better, *explores* – any general question, issue or problem that doesn't look as if it could be settled simply by observation, by calculation, or by reference to established fact. If the story explores an issue or prompts a question of this kind, then that question or issue is almost certain to be philosophical.

Philosophy is distinguished largely by the kind of interest that it shows in whatever topic it alights upon, and stories with a philosophical bent display the same kind of regard. Children's stories commonly involve problems or issues having to do with friendship, for instance, although they don't always treat the topic in a way that invites philosophical curiosity. Yet if a story explores the nature of friendship – of what it is to be a friend – or it raises questions about the boundaries between friendship and other relationships, then the treatment is bound to be philosophical to some extent. For example, there is a very simple story by Kerry Argent, called *Friends*, which tells us about Woolly Wombat and his friend Bandicoot.[1] In the story we learn that they live together, eat together, have fun together. Sometimes they fight, but they always make up. On the basis of this story, you could ask children whether friends always do these things, and whether there are people who aren't friends who also do these things. You could then go on to discuss what other things might help to constitute friendship. When raised for our reflective consideration, the questions 'What is a friend?' and 'How is friendship different from other relationships?' have the character to which I refer. They are general, open questions that are not settled by appeals to the dictionary, or to uncontentious, established fact. Someone who asks these questions can probably define the word 'friend' as well as the rest of us. What such a person seeks is deeper understanding, a more careful articulation of experience. In short, the questions point in the direction of inquiry – an inquiry in which both philosophy and literature have a share.

A story will have the philosophical content needed for classroom inquiry if it can be used to prompt these general, open questions. Let me reinforce the point with a few illustrations from elements of stories, each accompanied by three or four questions of increasing generality, taking us from the story to some philosophical topic. Each of these topics has been discussed at some point in the history of philosophy.[2]

Princess Smartypants Princess Smartypants turns a prince into a frog, so reversing the traditional role of the fairytale princess.

- How is Princess Smartypants different from most fairytale princesses?

- If a princess does not behave as she's supposed to behave, has she done something wrong?

- To what extent do you think we ought to behave in the way that is expected of us?

The Very Hungry Caterpillar One sunny Sunday morning a very hungry caterpillar hatches out of a little white egg and proceeds to eat his way through the week. Having chomped through every edible item that lies in his path and grown into a big, fat caterpillar, he turns his attention to building a cocoon. Two weeks later he emerges transformed into a beautiful butterfly.

- Was the butterfly the same living creature as the caterpillar?

- Will you be the same person as you are now when you grow into a man or a woman?

- What would make you the same person, or why would that person be different?

Whistle up the Chimney   Whenever Mrs Millie Mack throws old railway timber onto her fire, trains come whistling down the chimney, go through the house, and away into the night.

- What makes the trains come to Mrs Millie Mack's house?

- Can you usually tell in advance what effects something will have?

- Is it possible that the effects which something has could have been altogether different from what they are?

The Magic Pudding   Sam Sawnoff and Albert Barnacle introduce Bunyip Bluegum to a magic pudding, which always remains whole no matter how much of it you eat.

- Can you imagine how the pudding came to be whole when part of it was eaten?

- Can you imagine both, neither, or just one of the following?
  (1) Some of the pudding was eaten, but it was still whole.
  (2) Some of the pudding was eaten, but none of it was eaten.

- Are some things so impossible that we can't even imagine them happening?

Aldo   A lonely girl has just one very special friend called Aldo. Aldo is a secret friend who helps and comforts the little girl when she's frightened, lonely or sad. Some days the girl forgets all about Aldo, but she knows that he will always be there if things go wrong.

- What things make Aldo special?

- What makes someone a special friend?

- Have you ever had an imaginary friend?

- Is a make-believe friend really a friend?

Nowhere to be Found   When Tom is shopping in the marketplace with his mother, he loses his temper, goes off in a huff and becomes lost. Searching for the way back, Tom comes across a woman knitting who keeps losing the thread, a man lost in thought and another who has lost his memory. He finds a parrot who has lost his squawk, a sea captain who has lost his sea-legs and a fishmonger who has lost his sense of smell. At last he meets an old soldier, from whom he learns that he is Nowhere. But all is not lost. The soldier shows him how to find his way back to the marketplace.

- What things in the story have been lost?

- Can you explain what makes the various losses different?

- Can you explain the difference between the following:
    (1) Tom's mother was *nowhere* to be found.
    (2) Australia is *nowhere* near Mexico.
    (3) I have been trying to solve this puzzle for the past ten minutes, but I've got *nowhere*.
    (4) Victor is training for the swimming carnival because last term he came *nowhere*.

It is important to realise that philosophy can be playful, even mischievous, and therefore lots of fun. Nowhere is this more apparent than in the conceptual play and love of paradox that animates so many stories for the young. When the Cat in the Hat[3] leaves a great pink cat ring in the bath tub and is made to remove it, the children become frantic as he succeeds only in shifting it from one item to another around the house. Not admitting defeat, the Cat in the Hat seeks the help of a sequence of ever diminishing cats, each one related in the same way to the one that came before. Right under the hat of the Cat in the Hat, is Little Cat A, who needless to say has a hat on his head. And under that hat there's Little Cat B, and under his hat there's Little Cat C. Together they set to work on the job, but they make such a mess of cleaning things up that Little Cat C has to call on Little Cat D, and from on the top of D's head comes Little Cat E, and so on down to V, W, X, Y and Z! This wonderful regress of nested cats has by now moved the mess out of doors, turning the whole landscape pink. Can anything be done to clean it up? Well, what does Little Cat Z have on his head? He has VOOM! Yes, that will be the way out of this awful mess, and also out of the yawning regress every bit as mock-terrifying as the prospect of a world decked out in cat-ring pink.

Here's another example, this time from that time-honoured lover of conceptual play and paradox, Lewis Carroll:

> 'Did you say "pig," or "fig"?' said the Cat.
> 'I said "pig",' replied Alice; 'and I wish you wouldn't keep appearing and vanishing so suddenly: you make one quite giddy!'
> 'All right,' said the Cat; and this time it vanished quite slowly, beginning with the end of the tail, and ending with the grin, which remained some time after the rest of it had gone.

'Well! I've often seen a cat without a grin,' thought Alice; 'but a grin without a cat! It's the most curious thing I ever saw in all my life!'[4]

Quite so! Indeed, how could there be a grin and nothing but a grin, all by itself? It's like a wave without a hand, or perhaps a thought without a thinker! Such things amuse us with their delightful disregard for the limitations of a less poetic world. They present puzzles which help us to articulate the half-realised possibilities of our concepts. They are like so much gold on the page just waiting to attract a child's philosophical attention.

Openness to Inquiry

You should always look for stories that have an open-minded outlook on life, that will encourage children to puzzle and question, to hypothesise and explore. If the authors you choose are themselves questioning, curious, reflective and exploratory, they are likely to awaken these things in the children.

Inquiry is often represented in stories in some way, as in a quest, or in a mystery, problem or difficulty that the characters try to solve. Even if the action is not driven by inquiry, look through the dialogue and action for signs that inquiry is modelled in the text. Ask yourself whether the characters:

- show curiosity
- give reasons
- show puzzlement
- consider alternatives
- ask questions
- search for evidence
- look for explanations
- correct themselves.

This does not mean, however, that the characters need to be excellent or even competent inquirers. When Winnie-the-Pooh and his friends set out to look for Small (who is 'lost'), we can be sure that forgetfulness and lack of judgement will result in delightful misadventure.[5] Pooh forgets to ask what Small looks like. So he constructs a plan in which the first step is to look for Piglet (who will know about Small) in some otherwise unspecified Special Place. Luckily Pooh doesn't have to follow his own plan very far in coming upon Piglet. Not looking where he is going, Pooh presently falls down a hole right on top of him. He infers that Piglet's cries for help are his own, explaining the squeaky voice he can't control as evidence that he's had a Very Bad Accident. Of course it turns out that Pooh and Piglet had at some time dug the hole themselves as a trap for Heffalumps, although Pooh reasons that they must have fallen down a Heffalump trap for Poohs. A curious conversation then arises about how to deal with Heffalumps: Pooh devises a most implausible plan of action, upon which Piglet fondly improves in his own mind with just a pinch of self-deception. Sadly, Piglet's plan is promptly put to the test when Christopher Robin happens upon the hole and is mistaken for a Heffalump. And what in all this happened to the search for Small? It hasn't so much been abandoned as entirely forgotten. (The kind of thing which happens to us all, and to children most of all.) As luck would have it, Small is discovered on Pooh's back, and so everything turns out well. That is, everything turns out well except that nobody remembers to tell Eeyore to call off the search, and he goes on searching the forest for the next two days. This chapter from A. A. Milne's classic *The House at Pooh Corner* is an excellent example of inquiry for young children to think about just because of the things that go wrong.

At least since Aesop's fables, moral matters have formed a strand in children's literature. Choices imposed by a moral dilemma form one thread, the battle between good and evil is another, and the development of moral qualities, such as finding courage or gaining self-respect, is yet another. While ethics is an important area of philosophy, and should certainly be included in classroom inquiry, you need to exercise care in selecting material with a specifically moral focus, because writing of this kind is often meant to instruct.

Ethical inquiry is quite different from moral instruction. Ethical inquiry in the classroom is meant to help children think about ethical matters, to become more reflective about the ethical dimension of their lives; it is not concerned with imparting particular moral values or precepts. Rather than teaching children that this is right and that is wrong, in ethical inquiry we might consider a range of ideas about what makes an action right or wrong – whether it's the consequences which matter, or society's approval, or how the action stands in regard to some system of moral law. Rather than forcing children to a given moral conclusion, we would look at what can be said for different attitudes and values. If a story invites a question such as 'What is the moral?' or presents children with morally loaded dice, you should beware of it. Look for material which presents and explores different points of view, and allows children to come to their own conclusions. This is no more than to say that in the moral domain, as elsewhere, the materials you use must support the spirit of inquiry. For a version of Aesop's fables without the moral imperatives, see Tony Ross's cunning reworking of Aesop in his *Foxy Fables*; and for outright subversion of the original moral intent, see Roald Dahl's retellings of some traditional children's tales in his *Revolting Rhymes*.[6]

In addition to philosophical content and openness to inquiry, look for stories that contain plenty of dialogue. If the children are old enough, consider having them take parts for reading or acting out a sequence of dialogue. Dialogue can show people exploring their differences, reasoning with each other, exchanging ideas, building upon each other's thoughts, and all the things that you want children to do in their own discussions. If the dialogue is exploratory, if it involves deliberation, if it shows people thinking together, then it is a stimulus for the children to do the same. Of course, if much of the dialogue is between children, so much the better.

If you are using illustrated children's books, don't forget to think about the pictures. Do they express ideas? Are they evocative? Is there something to puzzle over? Imaginative illustrations can be an asset, and can provoke children to ask philosophical questions too. Consider a book such as Eric Carle's *I See a Song*;[7] apart from one introductory page with words, it is entirely composed of images. These wonderfully imaginative pictures take us into the realm of metaphor: music talks, you hear colours, they dance and so on. The book may suggest questions about the relations between art and music, and between the senses of hearing and vision.

By the same token, unimaginative illustrations will work against you. They can also be a drawback when children find that things are depicted differently from how they had imagined them. So think twice about a book that depends heavily upon pictures which don't leave much room for the children's imaginations.

Analysing the Text

Now let me take you through a text in order to show how I would approach it. It is a version of the story of William Tell.[8] I have marked up the text by indicating some significant incidents and ideas in the margin – what seem to me the kinds of things that might stimulate inquiry in the classroom, and which I could use to prepare exercises and discussion plans. It may be that you would select a somewhat different range of things, but so long as you keep your eye on the main concepts and leading ideas, your list is likely to be a good one.

I should add that the text was not originally designed for classroom inquiry, and it may not be the kind of text that you would choose. It is a folk tale and therefore presents complex historical events in a rather simplistic fashion. I have chosen it partly because it is a self-contained story that is short enough to include in a book such as this, but more importantly because of the number of philosophical themes to be found beneath the surface.

William Tell

A Tale from Switzerland

Do you know where Switzerland is? That's where I come from. My grandfather says that our family has lived in Switzerland for as long as anyone can remember.

being ruled by another country

harsh rule

Many years ago my country was ruled by a nearby country called Austria. In Swiss legend, the Austrian rulers are shown as cruel and brutal, and the Swiss are said to have often complained of the harsh treatment they endured. They longed for the time when they would be free.

self-determination

For many years no one was bold enough to stand up against the Austrian masters. Until at last their chance

*disobeying
orders*

*legend
national hero
glowing pride*

*different
perspectives*

came when a man named William Tell disobeyed an order of one of the governors, and then called on the Swiss to drive the Austrians out of the land. Many people say that no such person existed, and that the story of his life is only a legend. However, many Swiss people regard him as a national hero. They speak of him with glowing pride as someone who stirred up his people to free their land from Austrian rule.

Now I am going to tell you the story of William Tell and what happened so long ago. At least, it's one story about what happened. If I lived in Austria instead of Switzerland, then maybe I would tell a very different story about the same events. Maybe I would think about them in a different kind of way.

*   *   *

*injustice
being filled
with pride
Should we
always do
as we are told?
asking for
reasons
courage,
defiance
& pride*

One day a new governor named Gessler arrived from Austria. He was both harsh and unjust in his dealings with the Swiss. And he was so filled with pride that one day he placed his scarlet hat upon a pole in the market place and ordered everyone to bow to it as they passed.

Some of the people did as they were told. But the bold hunter William Tell, who was in the market place with his young son, would not do so.

'Why don't you bow like the others?' asked his son.

'Because I am not a slave,' he replied. 'The day will come when these tyrants will be driven from our land.' Then he lifted his head proudly and strode past the hat.

*   *   *

*being the
best
& reputation*

caution

When Gessler heard what had happened he was enraged and ordered Tell to be taken prisoner. Soon he and his son were brought before Gessler.

'What is your name, Switzer?' Gessler demanded.

'Tell is my name – William Tell.'

'Indeed. So you are Tell!' Gessler mocked. 'I've heard about you. They say you're the finest shot with the cross-bow in the land. Now, tell me – is that true?'

'Well – I've shot in competitions with many who are skilled at the bow,' Tell said cautiously.

wager

'I'd like to see you try your skill,' Gessler went on. 'More than that, if you can hit the mark I offer you, I promise we shall forget about the hat, and you shall go free.'

'By all means I'll shoot for you,' said Tell. 'What mark shall I take?'

'Is this your son?' Gessler inquired.

'Yes.'

'Is he a brave boy?'

'I think he is.'

Tell faces
a moral
dilemma

love, fear
and anger

'Good!' chuckled Gessler. 'Then he can help you. Let the boy stand in front of that great oak. Place this apple on his head. If with one shot you can hit the apple, then you shall go free.'

There were murmurs of surprise and horror from the soldiers. 'What!' Tell shouted. 'You ask me to shoot at my son, my only son? Never! Not for you or anyone!'

'Father!' called the boy.

'Yes?' said Tell, his voice shaking.

bravery
and trust

'Father, I'll stand straight and still. You never miss your mark. You can hit the apple, I know.' Tell said nothing. 'Give me the apple, please, sir.'

'Good, my boy!' chuckled Gessler. 'Good.'

'I'm ready, father.'

'Come, Tell!' said Gessler. 'This should be the greatest shot in the history of the cross-bow! . . . Why, he's taken two arrows from his quiver. I should have thought one would be plenty.' He chuckled again.

inference
faith
skill

Taking aim, William Tell whispered, 'Now, God be my guide.' T-w-a-n-g! Soliders gasped. A cheer arose.

'Thank God,' sighed Tell, 'my boy is safe.'

'A noble shot,' said Gessler. 'The apple's cut in two.' Then angrily he added, 'But what is this second arrow for?'

justice
and revenge
what is
treachery?

'For you,' Tell replied. 'If I had harmed my boy, this arrow would have pierced your heart.'

'Traitor!' shouted Gessler. 'Seize him, men. Hold him.'

*   *   *

bondage

Heavily chained, William Tell was dragged to a boat which was to take Gessler back to his castle. On the way a

skill

grasping freedom

taking revenge

fighting for freedom greater freedom

storm suddenly arose, and as Tell was the only one in the boat who knew how to steer, his chains were unfastened and he was allowed to take the rudder. Skilfully he guided the boat beside a ledge of rock near the shore. Then, before a hand could be stretched out to stop him, he leapt ashore and disappeared.

But he had not forgotten Gessler. He hurried to Gessler's castle, hid among the trees that bordered the pathway, and, when the governor rode by, he took careful aim and shot him through the heart.

The Swiss now decided to arm themselves and drive their enemies out of the land. Tell was made their leader, and several times he defeated the Austrians in battle. Although he was unable to drive them out of Switzerland altogether, his victories made them treat the people much better.

★   ★   ★

freedom of self-rule

William Tell lived on for many years, but in 1345 a great flood swept through the valley where he had his home, and he, with many others, was drowned.

About a hundred years later the Austrians were driven out of our country, and Switzerland was free at last.

★   ★   ★

a true story

different perspectives

That is the end of my story. As I said, many Swiss people think that it is a true story. But does that mean there couldn't be a different story about what happened? I'm not sure. What do you think?

This material is rich in concepts and issues that would make it suitable for inquiry. Among its leading ideas are the right to self-determination, the value of freedom, the evils of tyranny, and the power of the individual. Also apparent are the connections of injustice with revenge, of bravery with trust, and of love with courage. To take just one of these, look at the long list of vocabulary that has to do with some kind of freedom or its lack: *chained, disobey, dragged, drive out, free, governor, guide, hold, master, order, take prisoner, ruled, seize, slave, tyrant, unfastened.* Personal, moral and political freedom are woven together and touch nearly every incident in the story — as when Tell defies Gessler's order and refuses to bow to the hat, or he is taken prisoner and bound in chains, or is offered his freedom if he will accept Gessler's cruel challenge. Whatever its literary merits, this text would be quite adequate for classroom inquiry.

I will return to the story of William Tell in Chapter 5 and show you how discussion plans and exercises could be constructed for it. For the moment, however, I hope that you now have some idea of how to go about selecting story material for classroom inquiry.

NOTES

1. Kerry Argent, *Friends* (Ringwood, Victoria: Omnibus/Puffin, 1988).
2. The stories mentioned below are: Babette Cole, *Princess Smartypants* (London: Hamilton, 1986); Eric Carle, *The Very Hungry Caterpillar* (Harmondsworth: Puffin, 1974); Nan Hunt, *Whistle up the Chimney* (Sydney: Collins, 1981); Norman Lindsay, *The Magic Pudding* (Ringwood, Victoria: Penguin, 1957); John Burningham, *Aldo* (London: Jonathan Cape, 1991); Alan Marks, *Nowhere to be Found* (Saxonville, Maryland: Picture Book Studio, 1988).
3. Dr Seuss, *The Cat in the Hat Comes Back* (New York: Random House, 1958).
4. Lewis Carroll, *Alice's Adventures in Wonderland* in *The Complete Stories of Lewis Carroll* (London: Magpie, 1993), pp. 66-7.
5. A. A. Milne, *The House at Pooh Corner* (London: Methuen, 1928), Chapter 3.
6. Tony Ross, *Foxy Fables* (London: Puffin Books, 1987); Roald Dahl, *Revolting Rhymes* (London: Puffin Books, 1984).
7. Eric Carle, *I See a Song* (London: Hamish Hamilton, 1973).
8. The narrative has been adapted from A. E. Williams & C. Eakins, *New Social Studies through Activities* (Sydney: Martin Education, 1980), and appears by permission of Martin Education.

CHAPTER FOUR

Building a Community of Inquiry

Since philosophical inquiry may be new to you, this chapter will offer some advice about how to get underway in the classroom, and discuss the things that the teacher should be doing (or *learning* to do) in building a community of inquiry. I have tried to keep these suggestions brief and practical. Since many of them will mean more to you once you have had some experience, you should consider returning to this chapter once you have had the opportunity to put some of them into practice, or sharing your experiences with a colleague and then referring back to the book.

Getting Under Way

The basic arrangement recommended for philosophical inquiry is class discussion, interwoven with small group activity. By whole class discussion I do not mean a teacher-centred activity. Although the teacher needs to guide the discussion and model the procedures, the approach to philosophical inquiry is child-centred. It is important to appreciate this fact, and not to mistake the whole class nature of much of the inquiry for a session in which the teacher simply provides demonstrations. Having said that, let me make a few basic points about the recommended arrangements for getting under way, both with whole class discussion and small group work.

Arranging for whole class discussion

You need a suitable physical arrangement for whole class discussion. Children need to be facing each other, so that every child is able to see every other child's face. The best arrangement is to place the children in a circle, either in their seats or on the floor. A session can be as short as twenty minutes when you are starting out in the early grades, and some classes can go on for as long as an hour and a half in the upper primary school. In many cases, therefore, it is best to have the children in their seats. Don't allow children to sit outside the circle, or to form little corners, where they will not be full participants in the discussion. The common practice of grouping younger children on the floor in front of the teacher when reading stories is also not really suitable for our purposes. It is best to avoid a physical orientation towards the teacher.

Since you will also want to make use of small groups, try to have an arrangement in which children can break into groups and reform as a class with a minimum of fuss. The illustrations in this book will give you some idea of possibilities that other teachers have found to work well.

When conducting discussion with the whole class, position yourself in the group so that you can have ready access to the board, or to large sheets of butcher's paper, for writing up children's questions and working with exercises. Since it's desirable to leave children's questions up in the room between sessions, butcher's paper may provide the best option, provided that the sheets are large.

It is vitally important that all members of the class have the opportunity to enter discussion. Even with thirty children, a well-run discussion will provide opportunities for everyone to speak. Some teachers find this suggestion initially surprising, but experience with the kind of discussion recommended has shown that this is so, provided it is conducted with attention to the procedures described below.

If you would like to experiment with a smaller group, see if you can find another teacher or a parent to assist you so that the class can be divided into two. That will increase the time available for students to speak, as well as making it easier for you to conduct the session. Even if that isn't possible, once the class has some experience with the procedures, you might like to try dividing it into two for part of the discussion, one group working with the teacher and the other working independently, as you can see in the illustration on page 36. Some teachers find that this is surprisingly effective.

Working in pairs and small group discussion

Once children are used to the basic procedures of classroom inquiry, you can introduce small group work. Divide the class into pairs or small groups for devising questions. Ask each group to come up with its own questions, and then to select one of them to place on the board. This will produce a smaller number of more

The class has been divided in two for part of the discussion, one group working with the teacher while the other group works alone

considered questions for general discussion. On another occasion, divide the children into small groups for part of the discussion, and then have them report back to the class as a whole. By doing this, you will increase verbal participation and maximise the opportunity for the children to develop their skills. As you will see in Chapters 6 and 7, a great deal of the supporting work with exercises can also be done in pairs and small groups. This is useful both for reinforcement after discussion and sometimes as a preliminary to it.

Reading

Normally the class will begin a session by reading a story. If you are working with a short story, then read all of it. With some of the novel-length purpose-written materials, you may read just a section or two. You may be surprised at how little material children need in order to generate a healthy list of questions.

It is hard to give general advice about reading, since so much depends upon the age and composition of your class, and whether multiple copies of the story materials are available. If it can be arranged, the children should have access to the text, either through a 'big book' for younger children or through multiple copies in the older grades. If children are ready for it, then it is a good idea to have them read aloud to the class, either by taking a paragraph at a time, or perhaps by assigning

These children are engaged in a small group discussion. Later the class will consider the results of these deliberations

parts beforehand if there is dialogue. It is best if children prepare for reading by a quiet reading period or some other form of rehearsal, but however you handle it, the reading should be a shared activity in which the whole class is involved.

Setting an Agenda

Raising questions

Once you have finished reading, turn immediately to ask for questions about what has been read. On the first few occasions, begin by telling the children that they can ask about anything which they found puzzling, peculiar or odd in some way. They may like to question an action with which they didn't agree. There may be something that the story made them think about which they would like to discuss. As questions arise, write them on the board, numbering them as you go, and write the children's names after their questions to acknowledge their contribution. Sometimes it will be appropriate to ask a child what part of the story prompted a question. If the children have copies of the story in front of them, you can ask for the page number of the relevant passage and write it alongside the question for further reference. To give the general idea, here's a set of questions raised by a Year 5 class in response to a story of mine called 'Just Like Magic':[1]

The children's questions have been written on the board, and form the basis for class discussion. Note that related questions have been identified in the upper left-hand corner

1. What is fortune-telling if it isn't looking into the future? (Lienna, p. 75)
2. Should we believe in fortune-telling? (Petrov)
3. Why do we need fortune-telling? (Ivan)
4. How can something be *just like* magic? (Illya, p. 76)
5. Why does Brian think that Mr Magic couldn't be a woman? (Anna, p. 79)
6. If it was the back part of the lion, how could it speak? (Nadia, p. 74)
7. How did Mr Magic make his voice come through Reginald? (Nicholai, p. 78)
8. How could a person who believes in God also believe in magic? (Andrew, p. 73)

These children were having their first lesson in philosophical inquiry and the questions are fairly typical for their age group. They attend a state school in Moscow, as it happens, but their responses are not much different from those you would expect of children in Sydney or London.

After the children have become used to the practice of raising questions, don't forget that you may vary these procedures. For instance, as mentioned earlier, you can break the class into small groups and ask each group to come up with one question to write on the board. Or you can ask the children each to write down their own question, and then see which questions the class would most like to discuss. Do place the selected questions on the board.

These procedures need to be varied when working with very young children. While young children are perfectly capable of asking questions spontaneously, some of them may not readily distinguish between asking questions and making comments or statements if called upon to ask a question. If this happens, do encourage the children to begin simply by telling the class what they liked or found interesting about the story. Then help them to find a word or two which will identify their contribution, and write it on the board.

Even if you begin in this way, however, always encourage the children to ask questions. When a child remarks on something in the story, for example, you might say, 'Would you like to ask a question about that?' When it is appropriate, ask a child to attempt to turn his or her comment into a question. When someone asks a question, make the children aware of it and then immediately ask whether anyone else has a question. You might also consider having the children practise turning statements into questions.

Sometimes children of any age will have difficulty in formulating their questions. On such occasions, see whether there is someone else in the class who can assist. This is often the best option, because it encourages children to listen carefully to each other and to help one another when difficulties arise. If you need to assist more directly, then try doing so by asking the child to think about what he or she has said. If the child has made a statement that invites a question but cannot formulate it, sometimes it can help just to ask whether the question might begin with *how, why, what, who, when* or *where*. If the child has difficulty finding the right construction, you might formulate what you take to be the question and ask, 'Would it help if the question was expressed *this* way?' Again, you might point out that you are having some difficulty understanding *one particular part* of what a child is saying, so that you focus attention on what you take to be the problem.

Not all of the questions that children are likely to raise in the first lesson or two will lead to fruitful discussion. For instance, some of their questions may be matters of basic comprehension which are answered in the text, while others may have no very interesting answers in any case. Sometimes children will ask a question just to please the teacher, or in order to have their name on the board, rather than because of something that has sparked their interest. It is a good idea to deal briefly with these questions on the spot, so that the children begin to distinguish them from the kinds of questions that lead to inquiry. With a little experience, they will develop a sense of what is worth exploring.

Philosophical inquiry provides many occasions on which the children's insights will delight and surprise you. At the beginning, however, they may need some gentle guidance from you. If a child asks a promising question, draw attention to that fact. Other members of the class will soon see its appeal, and it will help them to ask better questions in turn. In the early stages, it is also better for the teacher to initiate discussion by choosing a promising question from the board, rather than taking a vote or asking the children to select a question with which to begin. This helps children to see what kinds of questions are likely to prove fruitful, as well as promoting good discussion.

Establishing connections

Often there will be significant connections between questions on the board. So ask the children whether some of their questions are about the same thing, or are otherwise related in a significant way. By grouping their questions, the children will be able to organise a basis for discussion. Look again at the list of questions raised by the children from Moscow:

1. What is fortune-telling if it isn't looking into the future?
2. Should we believe in fortune-telling?
3. Why do we need fortune-telling?
4. How can something be just like magic?
5. Why does Brian think that Mr Magic couldn't be a woman?
6. If it was the back part of a lion, how could it speak?
7. How did Mr Magic make his voice come through Reginald?
8. How could a person who believes in God also believe in magic?

Questions 1-3 on this list are connected because they are all about fortune-telling: what it is, whether we need it, and whether we should believe in it. That connection is at once obvious and useful for structuring discussion. By contrast, if a child were to claim that Questions 5 and 7 are connected because they are both about Mr Magic, that would be a superficial connection and not a good basis for discussion. It is therefore important for the class to attempt to distinguish between superficial relations of content and deeper, more interesting relations. This is not just for the sake of a productive discussion, but also because the deeper connections lie on the path that leads to philosophy. If you knew the story 'Just Like Magic', you would probably see that Questions 5 and 7 are related for a reason other than the super-ficial one suggested above. They are both about differences between appearance and reality – which is one of the story's central themes. Under that heading, the two questions have a much deeper, philosophical connection. (Can you see any other questions on the list which are also connected to that distinction?)

When a connection is established, ask the children to find a word or phrase to describe it, and then use that label to identify the group of questions on the board. It is also useful to have different coloured markers or chalk to identify each group of questions. This will help the children to organise their questions into possible agendas or lines of inquiry.

It is quite common for children to produce more questions than they can deal with in a single session. When it comes to discussion, don't rush through a group of questions, or cut inquiry off, because there are other questions that haven't been addressed. If the children are still very engaged in discussion, consider allowing the session to flow into the next teaching period. When you do draw a halt, you can ask the class whether they would like to continue the discussion next time and take up the remaining questions. Let the children's interest be your guide. Carrying questions over to another occasion will also give you the opportunity to plan some follow-up work in conceptual exploration or reasoning along the lines presented in the following chapters.

Conducting Discussion

Once you have organised your questions into an agenda, you will be ready to begin discussion. I will describe the teacher's role in discussion in general terms first, and say something about how to begin discussion. Later in the chapter I will return to many of these points in some detail, with examples.

The teacher's role

Your role in class discussion is in many ways akin to that of a conductor. You need to co-ordinate and enhance the performance. You may need to be vigorous at one moment, but restrained at another. You need to make sure that the children are listening to each other, and that everyone has the chance of being heard. You should also try to ensure that important themes are given appropriate treatment; and as the discussion proceeds, you might need to help underscore important developments and mark significant junctures. When children make mistakes, you may lead them through their thought again, and when some aspect of discussion is weak, you may introduce exercises to strengthen performance.

In conducting discussion, it is vitally important that you do not present yourself as the philosophical expert, or the subject authority, to whom the children turn in order to settle some difference of opinion. Your opinions, if you voice them, should have no special weight. If anything, this means that you should be very wary of expressing your views. Rather than being an expert in the content of the lesson, whatever it may be, your expertise lies in turning discussion to the best educational advantage.

Beginning discussion

Since the children's questions set the agenda, it is usually a good idea to call first upon the student or students whose question or questions have been selected to begin discussion. You can ask them to explain why they raised their questions if they haven't done so already, and they may need to explain more fully what they had in mind. They might have something to add about the connections that have been suggested with other questions, and they might also make suggestions about how their question could be answered.

By this time it is almost certain that several other children will have contributions to make. Allow several people to have their say, so that a discussion begins to take shape. You may find that the children have divergent opinions, that some actively disagree with others, or that they are willing to canvas a range of responses. In any case, they will quickly discover that it is not enough just to express opinions, or to make proposals of one sort or another. They may be called upon to give reasons for what they say. And since reasons, in their turn, may pull in different directions, and some are likely to be stronger than others, the children will find themselves in need of criteria by which to judge the outcome. Consequently you will need to ask children to support opinions by appeal to reasons, and you will often need to lead them through a search for criteria.

These are among the matters I will discuss later in the chapter. Before we go on, however, it might be helpful to look at a sample of classroom dialogue to illustrate a sequence of discussion. Let's take Lienna's question, 'What is fortune-telling if it isn't looking into the future?'

Teacher: Lienna, would you like to tell us why you asked your question?

Lienna: Well, in the story Brian says that the fortune-teller can tell fortunes, but she can't really see into the future. But you can't tell someone's fortune without looking into their future. That's what fortune-telling is.

Teacher: Thank you, Lienna. Would anyone like to comment on what Lienna has said? (*Pause.*) Yes, Ivan.

Ivan: What Brian's saying is that the fortune-teller can't really tell fortunes . . . because she can't really see into the future.

Lienna (pointing to the book): It says here, 'Perhaps she can tell a fortune,' said Brian, 'but she can't see into the future'. So Brian is saying that she can tell fortunes.

Nadia: He only says that *perhaps* she can tell fortunes.

Lienna: Okay Nadia, but what he *means* is that the fortune-teller might tell fortunes without being able to look into the future. I don't see how he can say that.

Teacher: Is that alright with you Nadia? Good. What about you Ivan?

Ivan: Um . . . I'm not sure.

Teacher: (*Pause.*) Can anyone else help out here? Yes, Andrew.

Andrew: I guess what Ivan was trying to say is that Brian means she can only tell *fake* fortunes. If she were telling real fortunes, then you're right, Lienna – she would have to be able to see into someone's future.

Teacher: Is that what you meant, Ivan?

Ivan: Yes.

Teacher: And do you agree with that, Lienna?

Lienna: I guess so. But telling fake fortunes isn't really telling fortunes. It's just pretending.

Teacher: Did you want to say something, Nadia?

Nadia: I agree that there's a difference between really being able to tell someone's fortune and making it up. So when Lienna says that fortune-telling is looking into the future, she's talking about real fortune-telling.

But when Brian says that the fortune-teller can tell fortunes, he's talking about fake fortunes – like Andrew said.

Teacher: So we have a *distinction* here – between real fortune-telling and fake fortune-telling or making it up, as Nadia said. Can anyone tell the class just what that distinction is? Yes, Nicholai, can you try?

Nicholai: In real fortune-telling you have to be able to see into a person's future, but in fake fortune-telling you just make it all up.

Teacher: Thank you, Nicholai. Did you want to add something, Anna?

Anna: Yes. I agree with what Nicholai has said, but I want to add that *all* fortune-telling is a fake. *No one* can really see into the future.

Petrov: I don't agree with you, Anna. Sometimes people can see into the future.

Anna: No, they can't.

Teacher: Petrov, you say that sometimes people can see into the future. Can you give us an *example*?

We will leave the discussion at this point. For the most part, as you can see, the teacher is asking questions. These have many functions, such as requesting reasons, seeking comment, checking for agreement, asking for examples and so on. At one point, the teacher notes that a distinction has been made. At the end, she is suggesting the need for an example. These are among the many things that I will begin to discuss in a moment.

As the children become practised in discussion, the teacher's role begins to change. The teacher will talk less. The children will ask questions of each other. They will draw distinctions and make connections for themselves. They will give reasons, explore alternatives, appeal to criteria and so on, with very little intervention. Yet there will still be much for you to do. Occasionally children will fail to see the implications of their views, or unwarranted assumptions may send them astray, and you may be able to help with an appropriate question. You should always help the class keep its bearings in discussion, see that everyone has a chance to participate, and help to ensure that mutual respect is maintained.

Although the forces within discussion are complex and its course is unpredictable, there are certain things that virtually assure success when it is in the hands of a skillful teacher. It takes practice to develop these skills, of course, and the courage to keep at it if things don't go quite as expected the first couple of times you try. Most of us can remember what it was like the first time we tried to drive a car in traffic. 'Next time try depressing the clutch before you change gear . . . If you're going to cut someone off, you could at least use your indicator . . . Turn left here. No *left* I said. *Left*! . . .' Until you have had some experience, you have to pay attention to so many things at once that it doesn't seem humanly possible to acquire the art. It can be much the same here. But you and your class will be learning all the while. So do keep trying.

Things to Bear in Mind

Having seen something of the conduct of discussion in overview, let's now look in more detail at some of the things that you should try to bear in mind.

Clarity

When conducting discussion, listen carefully to see whether you understand what each child is saying. If you are uncertain what a child means to say, then formulate what he or she has said as best you can and ask whether you have correctly understood. Or use some other probing question, such as:

- Do you mean that . . .?
- By . . . do you mean . . . or . . . or maybe something else?
- Would it follow from what you're saying that . . .?
- When you say . . . are you supposing/assuming that . . .?
- Are you saying the same thing as so-and-so, or maybe something different?

If it isn't clear whether a child has been understood by other children in the class, then ask someone who thinks they have understood whether they can tell the class what was said, or use questions like those above to probe understanding:

- Do you think that so-and-so means that . . .?
- Do you think it would follow from what so-and-so said that . . .?
- When so-and-so says that . . . do you think he/she supposes that . . .?

If you make probing questions such as these a regular feature of discussion, you will encourage the children to use them. Be ready to praise children who seek clarification by making a distinction, looking to a consequence or an assumption, or by trying to establish connections with what other children have said.

Consistency

Sometimes you will notice inconsistencies in what a child is saying, or between what is being said now and what was said earlier. Encourage children to look for consistency. If they unknowingly contradict themselves or appear inconsistent, draw your concern to their attention with a question such as:

- Can you say both that . . . and that . . .?
- Earlier I took you to be saying that . . . Now you seem to be suggesting that . . . Is that right?

More commonly, a group of children in dialogue will say or imply things that contradict each other. If the children do not deal with it themselves, be ready to intervene: 'Jesse, are you saying that so-and-so? . . . Well, Sarah was saying that such-and-such. Do you think it is possible that both of you are right?' In this way you will make it clear that you value consistency, and so you will encourage the children to pay due attention to it.

Don't forget that people who are just beginning to consider some matter need time to sort out what they think. They may say something when it occurs to them and later have second thoughts or change their mind. There is nothing wrong with that. It is a sign not only that children are thinking but also that they are beginning to *reflect on their thoughts*. In any case, to change your mind is not the same as contradicting yourself. I contradict myself if I hold that such-and-such is so-and-so while also holding that such-and-such is not so-and-so. But I do not contradict myself just because I began by saying that such-and-such is so-and-so and now I think that it isn't. This point is developed in the section below on 'Engaging in Self-Correction'.

Degrees of commitment

While everyone will know when someone is questioning something rather than affirming it, it may be less clear when someone is doubting something rather than rejecting it, or suggesting something rather than asserting it. When someone expresses doubt about a proposition, or raises objections to it, we are inclined to take this as rejection. When someone puts a proposition forward for consideration, or offers a conjecture, we may take this as support or assertion. No doubt such inferences exhibit a certain amount of savvy about human affairs, but we need to preserve these distinctions in a community of inquiry.

Children can assert, support, suggest, consider, wonder about, question, doubt, or reject a proposition. They can put it forward as a conjecture, or bet that it is true. There can be many degrees of commitment to an idea, and children need to distinguish between them. Once again, you can assist them by being ready to ask an appropriate question:

- Are you saying that circles can't ever have corners or that it's doubtful whether they do?

- Are you agreeing with Robert or saying that you think he is probably right?

- Do you mean that this is just another possibility or that it's more likely than the others?

Exploring disagreement

Disagreement plays an important role in inquiry. It brings children into dialogue, while presenting an issue or problem in a lively, dramatic form which heightens their interest. By interacting with one another over matters of mutual interest, children will really begin to think together. Through exploring disagreement and considering reasons that may be given on different sides of a dispute, they will become more reasonable in their dealings with each other. It will help to build both community and inquiry.

When disagreements occur in discussion, use the opportunity to help children acquire the habit of exploring different sides of an argument by giving reasons for what they say. First make sure that everyone knows what the disagreement is about. If necessary, ask the parties to restate their positions, or see if someone else can explain them to the class. Then ask the children to give reasons for their views. Ask those who hold one view why they think what they do, and then ask those with an opposing view to offer support for their opinion. Alternatively, ask children why they disagree with a particular view. Simple questions will get results:

- Why do you say that?

- Why do you think that you are right?

- What makes you think that she is wrong?

- Can you justify your answer?

When children disagree with one another, they will need very little encouragement to ask *one another* these kinds of questions. In disagreement, such questions come naturally. So make the most of it. We need to consider reasons when we think together, and this is an ideal opportunity to encourage children in the habit of giving and requesting reasons.

In exploring a disagreement, children will also need to *compare and evaluate* the reasons that they give. Again, a well-placed question is often all that is required:

- Why do you think that so-and-so is a poor reason?

- What if someone were to say that isn't a very good reason because of such-and-such?

- Do you think that such-and such is a good reason for believing so-and-so?

- Can anyone think of a better reason?

- Why is that a better reason?

- Would you say that, all things considered, we have more reason to think so-and-so than to think such-and-such?

In exploring disagreement, all the members of the class will have an opportunity to consider what can be said for or against one position or another. In many cases they will discover that it isn't simply a matter of one view being right while the others are wrong, and that there is legitimate room for disagreement.

Considering alternatives

Disagreements provide one kind of case where alternative points of view are expressed, but alternative perspectives and different possibilities can arise in many contexts of inquiry. In a police investigation or a commission of inquiry, for instance, there may be competing hypotheses to explain a given set of facts, and the detective or the commissioner will search for evidence in favour of one explanation or another. In a novel or a play, the writer will use characters and situations to explore the possibilities of human relationships and different points of view. Similarly, in philosophical inquiry the questions admit of alternative answers, and there may be many different points of view.

Classroom inquiry is an activity in which children are encouraged to look for alternative possibilities, and to be open-minded and flexible in their thinking. This is vital to good thinking in almost any field. Whether you are engaged in social science, personal development, or science and technology, you need to encourage it. If the class has become fixed on one idea, or alternatives have been neglected, you may need to ask whether anyone can think of a different approach or suggest another possibility:

- Does anyone have a different idea?

- How else could we look at this?

If all else fails, suggest another possibility yourself: 'How about such-and-such? Does that seem like a possibility?' Be slow to reach for this remedy, however, and never rush in to fill a gap or a silence with your own suggestions. Thinking takes time, and good reflective thinking can produce quite long periods of silence. Time youself. Wait for four seconds. If necessary, try waiting for *ten* seconds. Show the children that you know they need time to think.

Appealing to criteria

Criteria are the kinds of reasons to which people may appeal in making judgments, and to which they may refer in order to justify their decisions. Criteria include conventional standards by which things may be classified. For an establishment to be classified as a five-star hotel in a Michelin Guide, for example, it must meet certain standards. These standards are the Guide's criteria for placing an establishment under that classification. Criteria also include the standards that we use to evaluate actions and things in everyday life. If I say that the Thai Foon is an excellent restaurant, there will be criteria to which I can appeal – referring, perhaps, to preparation, presentation, atmosphere, service, and value-for-money – in order to justify or explain my judgement.

When there is uncertainty or disagreement about a judgement, it is often helpful to think about the criteria that would be appropriate to the case. If necessary, question the children about their use of criteria:

- Why (i.e. by what criteria) do you say that they are friends?

- If a person can't have a stone for a friend, why is that? That is, what criteria aren't met? (See *CRAZY CASE* in Chapter 6.)

- Since we don't seem to agree on whether dogs make better pets than cats, perhaps we could ask what different kinds of things we would each look for in a pet? That is, what criteria would we use?

You may be surprised at how often the questions that arise in classroom inquiry are tacit requests for criteria. We do not need to seek far for an explanation. Whenever we are faced with problems in choosing, evaluating, or forming a judgement of some kind, we need to consider what criteria can best guide our deliberations.

Do introduce the term 'criteria' to the children.[2] Even quite young children can handle it. It is essential to have names for our thinking tools, so that we know what to look for when we need them. Before long the children will be able to ask about the criteria they are using, and begin to examine their own judgements. As they gain control of this basic tool of reliable judgement, they will be taking an important step in the development of reflective thought.

Making appropriate distinctions

Misunderstandings and other problems can occur when we treat things as being much alike and overlook a significant difference, or when blinded by differences that are of little importance in the circumstances, we fail to see a genuine similarity. A young child who sees his mother crying when she is distraught may think that her pain is like that of a person who has met with an accident, without being fully aware of the crucial differences. One child who thinks about another primarily in terms of that other child's different ethnic background may fail to see that they both have common needs and feelings.

In classroom discussion you need to be aware when relevant distinctions are being made. When a child makes a useful distinction, try to keep it in play. If it is left idle when needed, draw attention to it with a question or a comment. If children neglect an important distinction, then be ready to assist:

- Is this case basically the same as that one?

- Given that these things are similar in many ways, can we think of some way in which they are different?

Children might also focus upon differences and distinctions and ignore significant similarities or connections. Again, a question from the teacher can help:

- Are these cases entirely different?

- Given that these things are different, can we think of ways in which they are very much the same?

Jumping to conclusions

If the first time I used Ace Airlines they lost my baggage, then I might jump to the conclusion that I am generally likely to lose my baggage on Ace Airlines and not fly with them again. My conclusion may be true, but my grounds are not compelling, and the *inference*, we might say, is tenuous. We all draw unwarranted conclusions from time to time, but it is a mistake to which young children are particularly prone: 'I was playing with the cat and he scratched me. He must be naughty.' 'Grandma and Grandpa have false teeth. When you get old, you have false teeth.' 'I lost the dollar that was in my pocket and Jason has a dollar on his desk. It must be my dollar.'

When children are jumping to conclusions, you may need to intervene with a question:

- Can we be certain that just because of so-and-so it must be the case that such-and-such?

- Does anyone know of a case where so-and-so occurs but not such-and-such?

- Is such-and-such the only reason why it is ever so-and-so?

This is quite an important topic, and in Chapter 7 you will find further discussion under the heading of 'Inductive Reasoning'.

Seeing implications

There are many occasions on which we may fail to see implications of one kind or another. We fail to understand what a statement entails, we fail to grasp what a speaker implies, we are blind to evidence that parades before us, or oblivious to the consequences of our actions. In all of these cases some meaning eludes us, or there is something that we fail to comprehend.

In talking about seeing 'implications', we should not inadvertently confuse such very different relations as logical implication, conversational implications, and implications of events and actions. However, I have drawn them together under the one heading here in the belief that all of our inferential habits belong to a common frame of mind, which classroom inquiry can help to develop. Let me say a little about each of them in turn.

Logical implication

The most part of what is normally taught as logic in universities deals with systems of deduction or logical implication. Such systems involve a great deal of formal reasoning that is not easily taught to children. Nevertheless, it is important that children should be aware that there are *logical* consequences as distinct from, say, practical consequences or causal consequences. Children in the middle and upper primary school can also make valuable use of some simple tools of deductive logic for thinking about predictions and explanations. So I have included some work on deductive inference under the heading of 'Hypothetical Reasoning' in Chapter 7.

Conversational implication

People may fail to infer what another's statement, command or question is meant to imply, so that they do not properly comprehend it. Often the circumstances or the tone of an utterance are supposed to make its implications clear. The question 'What is the milk jug doing on the table?' may mean 'It should be in the fridge.' The question is rhetorical, and both the questioner's tone and the circumstances may make its message clear. Yet this is not always so. As anyone who has travelled in a country with a different culture knows, it isn't just the struggle with vocabulary that can cause misunderstandings.

In a discussion dealing with logical possibility, one child said to another, 'Where would you find a round circle?' meaning roughly, 'There aren't any round circles.' Given that this was what the child meant, it's not very surprising that his utterance produced puzzlement. After a moment the teacher broke in with a follow-up question: 'David, are you saying that there are no round circles?' 'Yes,' he responded, 'because when you look very closely at a circle – any *real* circle – you will always find that it has little corners or wobbly bits, and so it isn't really round – not *perfectly* round.' David's meaning was now clear, and an interesting discussion developed about whether a circle is round *by definition*, whether the things we call circles really fit the definition, and indeed whether there really are any circles at all. This might have all been lost if clarification hadn't been sought and the implication of David's rhetorical question made clear. So be aware that children may be confused or puzzled because they fail to grasp such implications, either in discussion or in their reading. If you bear in mind what I said earlier about the need for clarity, you and your class will be paying attention to what is of primary importance for our purposes.

Implications of events and actions

Children should be encouraged to see what a set of circumstances portend, just as they should be encouraged to think about the implications of their own actions. Adults often become frustrated because children seem unaware of the possible consequences of what they are doing. 'Don't fill your glass to the rim.' 'Don't put your glass on the edge of the table.' But commands like these scarcely help a child to focus on the possible consequences. It would be better to ask: 'What could happen if you fill your glass to the rim?' 'What could happen if you put your glass on the edge of the table?' In other words, we should encourage children to consider the consequences of their actions.

Since stories present sequences of actions and events, they are a valuable resource for encouraging children to think in terms of causes and consequences. When the characters face a dilemma, or disaster threatens, or there is an unexpected turn of events, children's attention can be drawn to the implications. Don't miss the opportunity to talk about what might happen if you were to do *this*, what the children would do if faced with *that*, or what might have been done to avoid *the other*.

Engaging in self-correction

We are bound to make mistakes when we explore ideas. We may set out in the wrong direction, or take a wrong turning and become completely lost. We may fail to see landmarks, we may be drawn toward mirages, or stumble on doggedly over barren ground. As we become more practised in inquiry, we gain our bearings from one another and gradually we learn how to correct our mistakes. We listen to each other, we consider alternatives, become more aware of our assumptions and of where things lead. In the process we all become more reflective, less certain that we must be right, more prepared to acknowledge a mistake, and to allow ourselves to change our minds. Inquiry is a process that leads to *self-correction*.

In the classroom, children are engaged in self-correction when they wish to change the wording of their questions, or agree to qualify their remarks, or have second thoughts about some view they were defending. Be sure to acknowledge the children's attempts to correct their thinking. It will reward and encourage their efforts.

Sharing the discussion

Naturally some children will be more vocal than others, and the teacher needs to ensure that discussion doesn't become dominated by a relatively small group. Don't always direct your questions to the previous speaker or to the class as a whole. When appropriate, use *direct questions* to encourage other students into the discussion.

Often children who tend to be quiet have very worthwhile things to say. After a number of sessions, a child who has had little to say might offer a question to be put on the board. You should try to include that child's question in the discussion. A child who has not said anything in the first three sessions might now be ready to speak. If you regularly scan the class, you will quite likely become aware of this. Ask that child whether he or she would like to make a contribution.

Introduce a reflection time. It is quite common for quiet children to be more reflective. Make a space for them. Allow time at the end of discussion for anyone who hasn't made a contribution to offer comments or reflections.

Try to stay out of the discussion yourself as much as possible. Although in the early stages of building a community of inquiry you may find yourself having to intervene in the discussion more than you would wish, always try to keep a light hand on the rudder. Make sure that the children direct their remarks to one another, and not to you, and enter the discussion no more than necessary. As the children begin to internalise the procedures of discussion and become familiar with the basic moves, you will need to intervene even less often.

Respecting others

Every person engaged in a classroom inquiry needs to show respect for other people's thoughts and feelings. This involves listening carefully to what others have to say, not interrupting, waiting your turn, and not monopolising conversation. Respect is shown when people are willing to consider other people's points of view or they acknowledge other people's contributions. Respect doesn't require agreement, but it does require us to distinguish between criticising ideas and criticising persons. We may say, 'John, I think there's a difference between thought and feeling,' but not 'John, you don't seem to know the difference between thought and feeling.' As in any other classroom activity, it is the teacher's responsibility to ensure that the children are aware of these requirements. Of course, it is everybody's responsibility to see that they are observed.

Keeping your bearings

When groups of people get into conversation, they often meander from one topic to another without heading anywhere in particular. Listen to lunch-time conversation in the staffroom, or to a group of people talking at a social gathering, and observe the way the conversation moves. Classroom discussion aimed at inquiry moves in a different way. It centres on some question, issue, problem or idea, and the conversation builds around it. If we are talking about what makes someone a friend, say, or what it is for something to be fair, then the discussion is a persistent exploration of that concept. If we are looking at what makes a story good, or why we have babies, then the question gives the discussion its bearings. When we shift to a different topic, we ought to make that a conscious decision – not something we realise after the event, if at all.

In general, the teacher should try to see that the discussion forms a well-connected, integrated whole. You should always try not to lose sight of what's under discussion, and when necessary ensure that the children are mindful of the discussion's progress. This involves picking up on individual contributions:

- Can you connect what you just said to what we have been discussing?

- Does that help us with the problem we are looking at?

It includes inserting reminders or other indicators about general direction:

- How does what we have been talking about help us to answer Jackie's original question?

It can also run to closure and recapitulation:

- What did we discover today?

- What things did we talk about last time?

With a little effort, you and your students will learn to keep your bearings in a discussion. The main thing is to keep to the topic, so long as it remains of interest, and to keep trying to move the discussion forward.

It is often very useful to keep track of discussion on the board. Use coloured markers, arrows, connecting lines, and other diagrammatic devices to represent connections. Use a heading and list the points that the children have made or discussed as you go along, and encourage them to refer back to the board when necessary:

What is it for someone to be a friend?

Suggested criteria of friendship:

- living together
  Often friends don't live together.
  People who live together aren't always friends.
- playing together
  What about a pen-friend?
- being able to patch up differences
- trust

I'll end with a few more detailed comments on the idea of keeping track when the discussion changes focus, since a change in focus is often needed if we are to make progress, and it's at this point that an inexperienced group tends to get lost.

Keeping track of the main issue

To take up the example above, suppose that the class began by discussing the concept of friendship, trying to lay down some criteria for calling someone a friend. Let's say that some way into the discussion it becomes fixed for some time on the idea of trust. For the time being, it has narrowed its focus. The class shouldn't lose sight of the larger topic, however, and if necessary the teacher should see to it that the discussion makes its way back: 'How does what we have discovered about trust help us with our discussion of what makes someone a friend?' Once that connection has been made, the discussion can move on. Here again the teacher can help: 'What other things are part of being a friend?'

Moving from the particular to the general

Another common kind of movement is from the particular to the general – from examples, say, to a generalisation.[3] In response to the incident from *Alice in Wonderland* presented in Chapter 3, for instance, a child might have asked, 'How could the Cheshire Cat's grin remain behind when the rest of it had vanished?' Here the children might begin by talking about what makes up a grin, and whether a grin is the kind of thing that could appear on its own. Shortly, the discussion might turn to other things of this kind. Someone suggests the wave of a hand – just the wave, without the hand. Other gestures are mentioned. Someone else suggests a voice that cries out on its own. Could a voice exist on its own? What about a thought? Could a person vanish and just a thought remain? Here the children have broadened their focus to include other cases in an attempt to understand the mystery with which they began. They are discovering what gave the case of the Cat's grin its appeal. They are beginning to see the isolated grin as an enticing *example*, and may be on the verge of discerning just what it might be an example of.

This is the kind of movement you need to encourage. If the children had stuck with the grin and were having difficulty in dealing with it, you could try to move the discussion forward: 'Can anyone think of any other examples where it would be funny to say that something had vanished leaving just *this* behind?' Having explored a range of examples, then ask: 'Why are all of these cases so peculiar? Is there anything they have in common which could explain it?' This shifts the discussion to more general considerations which could help to enlighten us about the mystery with which we began.

This kind of move – from the particular to the general – is typical of philosophy. Seeing what things they have in common, comprehending the larger scheme of things, and discerning general principles – such endeavours provide one route to a deeper understanding.

This brings us to the end of a rather long chapter. Even so, much more could have been said, and I would encourage you to read further on the topic.[4] Also, as I mentioned at the outset, I suggest you return to this chapter once you have had some experience with conducting a community of philosophical inquiry in the classroom. It will help you to reflect upon your experience.

NOTES
1. In Philip Cam (ed.), *Thinking Stories 2: Philosophical Inquiry for the Classroom* (Sydney: Hale & Iremonger, 1994).
2. Don't forget that 'criteria' is plural. The singular form is 'criterion'.
3. See the section on 'Inductive Reasoning' in Chapter 7 for a discussion of generalisation.
4. For further reading, I particularly recommend the following: Matthew Lipman, Ann Margaret Sharp and Frederick S. Oscanyan, *Philosophy in the Classroom* (Philadelphia: Temple University Press, 1980); Gareth Matthews, *Dialogues with Children* (Cambridge, Mass: Harvard University Press, 1984); Ronald Reed, *Talking with Children* (Denver, Colorado: Arden Press, 1983); and Laurance J. Splitter and Ann Margaret Sharp, *Teaching for Better Thinking: The Classroom Community of Inquiry* (Melbourne: Australian Council for Educational Research, forthcoming 1995).

CHAPTER FIVE

Preparing Discussion Plans and Other Aids

Although you should begin a discussion with children's questions and comments, you would do well to supplement them with prepared plans and exercises in order to extend and help structure the discussion. This is one advantage of beginning with purpose-written materials. They provide you with ready-made exercises, activities and discussion plans. By working with these materials you will learn how to structure discussion, and they will also give you many ideas for other activities based on your own choice of literature. Even so, you can gain some insight into the conduct of classroom inquiry just by seeing how these aids are meant to function, and so at this point it will be helpful for us to look at some discussion plans and exercises.

Discussion Plans

Once a discussion is under way, the teacher may need to help give it structure and focus. An ethical issue might need to be carefully explored, for instance, or the discussion may circle around some concept that demands more direct attention. In these circumstances, it is useful for the teacher to have prepared some well-chosen questions to help guide the inquiry. A discussion plan is a carefully considered sequence of questions which does just that.

Teachers with a gift for discussion may rely on generating appropriate questions as it proceeds, but most of us need a plan. If you wish to prepare a plan before you have seen how the children respond to the story, then you will need to choose the most salient ideas. Ask yourself what incidents, issues or other aspects of the story are likely to attract the children's attention. Take two or three of the most likely ones and develop your plans around them. However, a more economical way of working is to do the reading, question-raising and agenda-setting in one session and leave the discussion for the next occasion. That gives you the opportunity to plan around the children's expressed interests.

A discussion plan will start with some incident or incidents in the story, or one of its leading ideas, and explore the issues or concepts involved. Let's go back to the story of William Tell related in Chapter 3 and look at some examples. As we saw, the concept of freedom is central to the story, and it would almost certainly arise at one point or another in discussion. There are several incidents that could be the basis of a question about freedom. For instance:

- William Tell chose not to bow to Gessler's hat. Does that mean he was free not to bow to the hat?

- In the end Tell chose to shoot at the apple. Does that mean he was free not to shoot at the apple?

- Tell explained to his son that he didn't bow to the hat because he was not a slave. Does that mean he was a free man?

- When Tell escaped from Gessler's boat he was free. Does that mean he was a free man?

These questions would help to focus discussion on contexts in which we speak of personal freedom of one kind or another, and by investigating these different contexts children may be led to consider a variety of answers that could be given to the more general question: 'What is it for a person to be free?'

Freedom of the individual is perhaps less at issue in the story of William Tell than freedom on a larger scale. Here are a couple of questions that might be raised:

- After Tell's victories over the Austrians the Swiss were treated much better. Does that mean they had more freedom than before?

- A hundred years after Tell's death Switzerland became free. What does that mean?

These questions invite children to think about social and political freedom, and take the discussion toward broader questions, such as:

- Could one country be ruled by another and still be free?

- Could a people have their own rulers and yet not be free?

Such a line of inquiry might even bring us to consider how a country is distinct from a nation, or whether a nation might be distinguished from a people, or a people from some other group, and what it could mean for any one of these entities to be free. Even if the discussion stopped far short of this, merely by moving in the direction of these more general issues you would help the children not only to think about freedom in the context of the story, but also to reflect on what it could mean to say that a person is free, or what it is to live in a free society or a free country. Such questioning is Socratic, meaning that it begins with the children's tacit understanding of freedom and attempts, through discussion, to make it explicit and articulate.

In a similar vein, we can use questions to help children explore the ethical dimensions of the story. For example, when Gessler challenges Tell to shoot the apple from his son's head, Tell faces a moral dilemma. Should he risk his son's life, or throw away the opportunity to go free? What should he do? Let's see if we can construct a sequence of questions that would help children explore the issue:

1. Why did William Tell at first refuse Gessler's challenge to shoot at the apple?

2. Why did Tell's son agree to Gessler's challenge?

3. What would you do if you were in William Tell's situation?

4. Was it alright for Tell to shoot at the apple when his son agreed to it?

5. Should Tell have left himself in Gessler's hands rather than taking the risk of harming his son?

6. Would Tell have been right to kill Gessler if he had missed the apple and harmed his son?

If you tried to think through Tell's dilemma, you might come up with a somewhat different sequence of questions. The questions I have chosen don't represent the only path through the problem. Even so, notice that they lead the discussion from the reasons that people in the story may have had for their decisions or actions, to what the children would have done in the situation, to what it would or would not have been right to do. In other words, the questions gradually ensure that the discussion moves onto ethical ground.

As I suggested in Chapter 4, classroom inquiry commonly moves from the particular to the general. We may begin by asking why someone in the story doesn't go by their real name, for example, and move to asking what makes a name a person's real name, only to end up by looking at what makes something real. Discussion gravitates to the philosophical. Since it is the deeper, more general, philosophical issues that get children thinking and that ultimately sustain their interest, this kind of movement is to be encouraged, and a good discussion plan can assist in the process.

Let's look at an example. As you'll recall, Gessler had issued a command that the Swiss were to bow to his hat, but Tell refused to obey. We can use this incident to build a set of questions that could help children think about rights and obligations in relation to commands. The questions move from the motivation of characters, to their rights and obligations in the circumstances, to a pair of general questions about obligations to obedience and the right to disobey:

1. Why do you think Gessler made people bow to his hat?
2. Why did Tell refuse to bow to Gessler's hat?
3. Would you have refused to bow to the hat?
4. Did Gessler have the right to issue such a command?
5. Did Tell have an obligation to obey the command?
6. When do people have an obligation to obey commands?
7. When do people have the right to disobey?

The character of the questions in a well-considered discussion plan leads children to think about the issues because the answers that may be given to most of them are not settled in advance. They give scope for genuine inquiry, in which children can explore and reflect upon ideas. By leading children into such discussion, we contribute to their moral education – not through moral instruction, but by helping them achieve a better understanding and awareness of such complex matters through inquiry. By having children discuss the social and political issues that arise from a story such as that of William Tell, we can guide them deep within the territory of social studies. With appropriate material in hand, we can do the same for other curriculum areas.

Exercises & Activities

Let us continue with this philosophical overture to William Tell by seeing how we can devise exercises to connect some of the deeper issues in the story with children's experience. Take tyranny, for instance. In order to set children thinking about such a thing, we would do well to draw upon things that are familiar. Fortunately, tyranny as absolute rule, or harsh and oppressive government, is beyond the experience of most children in our schools – although not all. In any event, tyranny as the arbitrary or oppressive exercise of power may be all too familiar to a larger number. So perhaps we can find things within many children's experience which are sufficiently analogous to the political condition for the children to use them as a basis for initial exploration. Here is an exercise that attempts this task. It is the kind of thing that could be photocopied and used directly in a whole class discussion, or introduced first for a preliminary discussion in small groups. You could even get children to think about some of the questions on an individual basis first, and then have a class discussion:

CONCEPTUAL EXPLORATION: Like a Tyrant

In the story, William Tell refers to Gessler and the Austrian rulers as tyrants, and Gessler is described as unjust and harsh. From your knowledge of the story, would you say that in the following cases someone is acting like a tyrant, or not? In some cases, perhaps you can't be certain. In each instance, can you explain the reason for your answer?

	Like a tyrant	**Not like a tyrant**	**Can't be certain**
1. The children in our street formed a club, but I don't like it any more because Peter made himself the leader and forces everyone to do just what he wants.			
2. Maria is always bossing her little sister.			
3. Our teacher is Mrs. Grimshaw. She's very strict.			
4. Anita doesn't like her boss at the supermarket. He makes her work terribly hard and pays her hardly anything.			
5. Every day before Laurie goes to school he ties his dog to a post in the back yard.			
6. Bill's father often threatens him when Bill doesn't do as he is told.			

An exercise of this kind moves us beyond the word *tyrant* as an item of vocabulary to the exploration of a concept, in terms of a group of possibly analogous cases. Notice that I say *possibly* analogous, because not all of the cases up for discussion are unquestionably so. Some cases lie at the margins of the conceptual domain, where what we should say is not so clear. They present the boundaries of the concept as uncertain, perhaps problematic, and as requiring a search for meaning.[1] This feature of the exercise helps to ensure that it meets our educational objective. By including cases where children will be less certain – where they will tend to disagree with each other, where they will have to consider what others say, where they may have second thoughts, where they may change their minds as discussion proceeds – we will encourage them to think.

Exercises in conceptual exploration can be used to help children see connections between items in their vocabulary. The following exercise is designed to encourage children to make such connections, here under the headings of FREE and NOT FREE. As I have set it out, it is an exercise prepared for individual work as a follow-up to class discussion:

CONCEPTUAL OPPOSITION: Free and Not Free

Below are some sentences relating to the story of William Tell, together with a list of words. Join each sentence to the word that could best replace the underlined word in the sentence.

Switzerland was once <u>ruled</u> by Austria.	rid
The Swiss longed for a time when they would be <u>free</u>.	forced
Tell wanted to <u>free</u> his land of Austrian rule.	captive
Gessler <u>ordered</u> that everyone should bow to his hat.	release
Tell was taken <u>prisoner</u>.	bound
Gessler agreed to <u>free</u> Tell if he could hit the apple.	governed
Tell was heavily <u>chained</u>.	unfastened
Tell was <u>dragged</u> to the boat.	demanded
Tell was <u>freed</u> from his chains.	liberty
Switzerland had gained its <u>freedom</u> at last.	independent

Now group the list of words on the right under the headings of FREE and NOT FREE. If you are uncertain about a word, then place it under the question mark:

FREE	NOT FREE	?
rid release unfastened liberty independent	forced captive bound	governed demanded

---

As a variation on this theme, you can ask children to construct the sentences themselves and then work with each other to look for synonyms. You will find this variation described under the heading *SWAP* in Chapter 6. For a tool that can assist with the exploration of conceptual oppositions, see *DUMBBELLS* in the same chapter.

If we are to encourage children to think well, we must also strengthen inferential habits such as seeing consequences, uncovering assumptions, and inferring motivation from action and circumstance. Exercises with this aim can readily be drawn from narrative material. In the case of William Tell, you could easily devise an exercise in inferring motivation by asking children to say what they think would be the most likely reason for actions such as the following:

- Gessler makes the Swiss bow to his hat.

- Gessler challenges Tell to shoot at the apple.

- Tell refuses to shoot at the apple.

- Tell's son agrees to Gessler's challenge.

- Tell's son stands straight and still.

- Gessler orders his soldiers to seize Tell.

- Gessler orders Tell to steer the boat.

- Tell kills Gessler.

This kind of exercise could also be used as a written follow-up activity for older children.

Finally, since the tools of philosophical inquiry have wide application, they can not only promote thinking in such areas as social sciences, science and technology, literature, and health, but they can also provide a bridge from one area to another. For illustration, let's take an exercise in making distinctions based on the story of William Tell – where the focus so far has been upon social studies – and use it as the basis for an art activity. We could pick any number of topics from the story, but the one I like the most is pride.

We speak of pride in many ways, and some of them can be found in the story. The Swiss are said to speak of their national hero with glowing pride. They take pleasure and rejoice in him. Gessler is said to be filled with pride. Children might say that he is full of *himself*. We might say that he is arrogant. And William Tell is described as raising his head proudly when he strides past the hat. He has a sense of his own worth and isn't going to lower himself by bowing to it. You could ask children to find the places where pride is mentioned, and then they could discuss whether the pride is different in each case. You could also ask them to distinguish between taking pleasure in something, being full of yourself, or having a sense of self-worth in a range of made-up cases, such as in the exercise on Pride' (see p. 62).

Once the children have had the opportunity to think about the matter and have begun to make some distinctions, you could ask them to make a picture of their choice to show one of the following: the harsh and cruel Gessler, filled with pride; William Tell as the Swiss national hero regarded with glowing pride; or William Tell lifting his head proudly as he strides past Gessler's hat. Afterwards there can be a class discussion of the children's work to explore the ways in which these different forms of pride have been given pictorial expression.

MAKING DISTINCTIONS: Pride

How do each of the following cases relate to the forms of pride identified in the headings below? Some cases might belong to more than one heading.

	Taking pleasure in something?	Being full of yourself?	Sense of self-worth?
1. Isabel takes a pride in her work.			
2. Lying is not something of which you can be proud.			
3. Stephen's snigger wounded Silvia's pride.			
4. Pug is the proud mother of three puppies.			
5. Matthew is too proud to admit his mistake.			
6. Swallow your pride!			
7. Giovanni is his mother's pride and joy.			
8. Penelope is as proud as a peacock.			

Although this excursion into the topic of discussion plans and exercises has been brief, it should give you some idea of how a plan can help to focus discussion on a particular concept or assist in the exploration of an issue, and how exercises may be devised for such activities as exploring conceptual boundaries, making conceptual connections, giving reasons, drawing inferences, and making distinctions. As I said at the beginning of the chapter, one advantage of gaining some experience with purpose-written materials is that they make you more conversant with these aids.

If you are using material that you have selected yourself, do work through it in the way that I suggested in Chapter 3, and try to develop one or two sets of questions around the leading ideas before you try to conduct discussion. With a little thought you will be able to develop useful sequences of questions, and with practice you'll get even better at it. If you have the time to devise some exercises, try your hand at that too, and here the tools described in the next two chapters should be helpful.

NOTES

1. Concepts which invite philosophical exploration are typically of this kind. In Chapter 6 you will find a thinking tool called *TARGET* which is specifically designed to help children explore conceptual boundaries.

PART III

Tools for Thinking

CHAPTER SIX

Conceptual Tools

Good thinking is an art rather than something accomplished by the routine application of tools. Yet we all need tools in order to think effectively, and as with learning the art of cooking, those who are learning the art of thinking will need some basic tools and practice in their proper use. The most accomplished chef learnt this way. It is no different with thinking.

In this chapter we are going to cover some simple tools of categorical thinking for exploring concepts, defining our terms, and sorting things into classes. Most of these tools have been designed primarily for group work and class discussion, but they can be adapted for individual use. As the children find their way in philosophical inquiry, the teacher who has some familiarity with these tools will begin to recognise many opportunities for their introduction. There is no particular order in which they should be introduced, and usefulness for the purpose at hand is the basic criterion to employ. All the same, I would suggest that you introduce them one at a time. When the children have become familiar with one tool, then you can look for the opportunity to introduce another one. I will explain the purpose of each tool as we go along, and show you how it works in the classroom.

Exploring Concepts

Concepts make intellectual knowledge and understanding possible. They underpin language and inform both perception and action. We can see this by way of an example. Suppose that at five years of age, Thomas has very little conception of what it is to be proud. That being so, he will not be able to decipher the pride that is written on another child's face, cannot aim to be proud of his efforts, and certainly cannot understand that pride is not always a virtue. For Thomas, the word 'pride' will have no clear meaning, it will not be part of his working vocabulary, and he will have difficulty in using it to form a sentence.

People's thoughts and actions reflect the richness, diversity, coherence and integration of their concepts. To the extent that we lack conceptual diversity, our thought is restricted; when our conceptual structures are rudimentary, so are our thoughts; when our concepts lack coherence, our thought is conceptually confused; and when we fail to make firm connections between our concepts, more complex meanings elude us. Let's take pride again. As adults we all have an understanding of pride, of course, and unlike Thomas we know that it is not always a virtue. Yet we might not quite understand what could be meant by 'burning pride', or be able to connect pride with other psychological attitudes and people's feelings, so as to fully comprehend the meaning of these lines from Sir Walter Scott:

> Vengeance, deep-brooding o'er the slain,
> Had locked the source of softer woe;
> And burning pride and high distain
> Forbade the rising tear to flow.

Unless we possess fairly sophisticated concepts, we cannot understand such language, let alone use it.

A classroom teacher must promote children's conceptual development in every area of the curriculum. So the effective teacher is always making use of opportunities to build concepts. Besides attending to concepts in the various learning areas, however, *we also need to encourage children in the kinds of mental habits that promote conceptual development*. It is not enough just to teach specific concepts. We also need to enhance the children's capacity to acquire concepts and to enrich them. The tools described below have been designed with that end in view.

It is commonly thought that conceptual facility is essentially a matter of inherent ability, so that there is little we can do to improve someone's performance at conceptual tasks. This is a mistake. Just as we learn to use a diary as an aid to memory, so we can learn to use conceptual aids. Diaries help us to remember things that we would otherwise forget, and conceptual aids help us to extend our powers of conception. As teachers, we may not be able to do much about the inherent abilities of our students, but we can make the most of their capacities by providing them with tools and getting them into the habit of using them.

I have included five tools for conceptual exploration. For easy reference, I have called them *TARGET, CRAZY CASE, SWAP, BRIDGE* and *DUMBBELLS*. Use these names in the classroom, so that the children have a tag with which to identify their tools. After a while children will know how to use them in discussion, and they can simply say 'Here's a crazy case' or 'Let's try a target'.

TARGET

TARGET[1] is a tool that children can use when they are uncertain about the nature of some concept or when a disagreement has arisen because a concept has vague or uncertain boundaries, as here:

> *Gino:* I wouldn't say that Princess Smartypants is beautiful.
> *Verity:* Maybe she's pretty.
> *Garry:* Could we say that she's attractive?
> *Helga:* Isn't being attractive much the same as being beautiful?
> *Amanda:* Maybe *attractive* is more like *pretty*.

With *TARGET* children pool their vocabulary to create a conceptual cluster, and then explore the cluster's conceptual boundary, trying to resolve disagreements by appeal to criteria. It can be applied to most concepts that have attracted the attention of philosophers, such as *good, true, beautiful, fair, right, person, possible, real, exist* and *know*.

Procedure

1. Have the class think of as many words as they can which they associate with the target concept. This step should be carried out quickly, without discussion. Don't reject any child's offering, and write each word on the board as it comes up. It can be useful to add a carefully chosen word or two yourself.

2. Divide the class into pairs and give each pair a blank target sheet, with two concentric circles, as in the example given for illustration. (Alternatively, of course, you could ask children to draw the circles for themselves.) Ask them to write each word on the list in what they take to be the appropriate circle, placing any words that they are uncertain about in the question-mark ring. If there are any words which they feel definitely do not belong to the concept, then they should be placed outside the circles altogether.

3. Now prepare for class discussion of any words that anyone considered writing in the question-mark ring. Go through the list on the board in order to have the class isolate these words. Make a target on the board and place the problematic words in the question-mark ring.

4. The discussion should then *identify and evaluate reasons* for retaining them in that group or moving them to the centre, or to the outside. (Reasons can

include examples, counter-examples and definitions, among other things. Definitions are discussed in the next section of this chapter. For counter-examples, see Chapter 7.)

Example

Target Concept: Knowledge

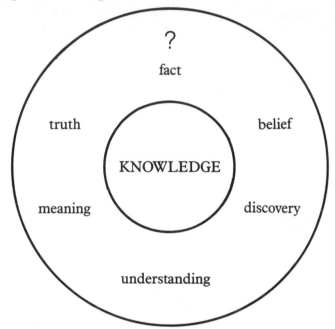

At the completion of Step 3, the words above have all ended up in the question-mark ring. Here are some highlights of the ensuing discussion:

Rebecca: To *discover* means to come to know something. So *discovery* belongs to the knowledge circle. [Rebecca is using a definition.]

Scott: Belief should be placed outside the circles altogether. It isn't the same as knowledge. Once people believed that the earth was flat, but later they discovered that it isn't. So just because you believe something doesn't mean that you know it. [Scott is offering a *counter-example* to the claim that belief is knowledge.]

Lydia: I don't altogether agree with Scott. People's beliefs can also be true, and then we would say that they *know* that thing. Like knowing that the earth is round, for example. That's a true belief. The things that you know are the things that you believe which are also true. [Here Lydia is offering a *definition*.] So I think that 'belief' should stay where it is – it's connected with knowledge.

Amanda: Understanding belongs with *knowledge*. Like if I understand a word, I know what it means. [Amanda is offering an *example*.] It's the same thing.

Eugenio: I agree with Amanda. If you understand something, then you know what it means, and if you know what it means then you understand it.

CRAZY CASE

In *CRAZY CASE*[2] children think up unlikely, bizarre or impossible cases for the application of concepts. Since odd or crazy examples can help us to discover the criteria that we normally use when applying a concept, *CRAZY CASE* can be introduced whenever children need to clarify those criteria. For example:

Tom: I know someone who made friends with a clock.

Katrina: There's a person in the park who is made out of rock.

Tom's case highlights the concept of friendship, and Katrina's case picks out the concept of a person. Once children grasp the idea they will introduce it themselves quite readily.

Procedure

1. Have someone invent a crazy or silly case to apply the concept in question.
2. Now have the class say what is crazy about the example. As discussion proceeds, list the children's reasons on the board:

What's crazy about a person being made out of rock?

- rock isn't living
- rocks can't think
- rocks can't feel
- rocks don't . . .

The list should provide a reasonable set of criteria for applying the concept. That is to say, it will include at least many of the features or characteristics that something either must have, mustn't have, or will normally have if the concept can be applied to it. Don't be surprised if someone disagrees that a case is altogether crazy, and allow the discussion to linger on any contentious claims.

SWAP

SWAP is a way of discovering the array of meanings that a word can have when we use it in different linguistic contexts. It also makes children more aware of the conceptual relationships between groups of words. In *SWAP* children construct sentences using the word in question and then look for synonyms with which they could replace it. When using *SWAP*, be sure to choose words that have a rich variety of uses. Here are some examples: *agree, care, connect, different, free, good, mind, think, wrong.*

Procedure

1. It's a good idea to allow your students to use word building in *SWAP*, so begin by asking them to help you construct a list of words with the same stem that they can use. For *free*, this would include *freed, freely, freedom,* and so on. Write these words on the board.
2. Have each student construct a sentence for one or more of the words on the list.
3. Now divide the class into small groups and have each group look for a word or phrase for each of the sentences constructed by the children in that group which could replace the original word without substantially changing the meaning of the sentence. (A good test of whether the replacement will work is to rewrite the sentence with the new word or words in place of the old one. This can be demanding, so circulate around the class and assist in discussion where help is needed. You might consider having the children carry out this work on the computer.)
4. Re-form the class, and have students report back on all the replacement words that have been found. Use your judgement in allowing for discussion, and list all of the successful replacements on the board. (You can also put on the board some of the sentences that caused difficulty and ask for suggestions over the next day or two.)
5. Sometimes the words that have been discovered can be broken into interesting groups. So do think of asking whether the children can see any connections or distinctions among their replacement words.

Example

'Different'

Word list: different, differ, differing, differed, difference.

1. A cat is quite *different* to a dog. (dissimilar)
2. The Queen had a *different* crown for every occasion. (separate)
3. Jack grew so fast that Grandma could see the *difference* every time he came to visit. (change)
4. Why do you and your brother always have to *differ*? (disagree)
5. You should wear a *different* shirt. That one's dirty. (another)

A prepared set of cards are being used to form a bridge in this small group activity

6. My big sister has started wearing a ring through her lip. Boy is she *different*! (unusual)
7. Mr Bungle's feet are *different* sizes. (unequal)

BRIDGE

BRIDGE[3] helps to sharpen vocabulary and encourages children to make more precise judgements. It can be used with all those concepts that incorporate opposites – such as the concepts of temperature (hot and cold), size (large and small), beauty (beautiful and ugly), and emotion (happy and sad) – where children can use their vocabulary to build a bridge between the ends of the spectrum. I will describe *BRIDGE* as it is used for class discussion when some conceptual opposition needs to be explored. But you can also turn it into a small group activity by preparing sets of words on cards and asking the groups to order the words in their set to form a bridge.

Procedure

1. Write the words for the pair of opposites on either side of the board and draw a line connecting them. Have the children name the conceptual scale. Be sure that the opposites do actually lie towards each end of a conceptual scale

(like *hot* and *cold*) and are not merely conventional opposites (such as *cat* and *dog*).

2. Now invite children to supply words that fall somewhere along that line. When they offer new words, the children should attempt to say where to place them between other words that have been suggested. This may require some discussion. Keep going until the class runs out of words. You may need to remind the children that the words which mark opposites aren't always at the extreme end of the scale.

Example

snail's pace   crawl   dawdle   plod   walk   march   hurry   trot   rush   run   speed   race   rocket   like lightning

SLOW   FAST

Concept: SPEED

DUMBBELLS

DUMBBELLS is a simple device for building conceptual awareness through oppositions. It can build upon any of the conceptual oppositions that you might use for *BRIDGE*. Use it to help children associate their vocabulary with conceptual clusters.

Procedure

1. Begin with the pair of opposites that has come up in discussion (as in *BRIDGE*) only this time place them in the circles of the dumbbells.
2. Now ask the children to think of any other words that are similar in meaning to either of the words already on the figure. When a word is suggested, it is often useful to see if anyone can think of another word that would mean the opposite of that word. Place it in the other circle. Keep going until you run out of words.

Example

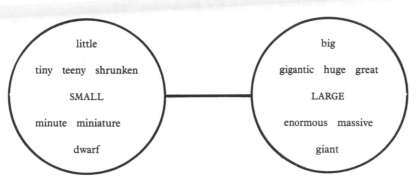

Definition

We often use words quite adequately without being able to formally define them. Someone who can reliably use a word in ordinary speech, and employ it in appropriate sentence construction, has a grasp of its meaning that is adequate for most purposes. All the same, there are occasions when we need to define our terms. Well-defined terms are required for technical and scientific purposes, for example, and in such specialised fields as medicine and law. In everyday discussion, people can misunderstand each other or get stuck on some issue simply because they are using terms without a clear or agreed definition. Moreover, people sometimes manipulate words to suit their purpose, which can mislead the unwary. Politicians and estate agents are often stereotyped as exponents of this device, but most of us resort to it from time to time. Those who know how to define terms are likely to be more critical when they encounter such ploys.

Therefore, just as students should be taught how to use a dictionary, so they should be taught how to define their terms. Learning how to define one's terms is not the same as learning definitions. Defining is a categorising task, which requires us to discern relationships between classes. In the simplest case, a definition specifies two partly overlapping classes, such that the term in question refers to things that are members of both classes. One will be the wider class, or *genus*, to which things of that kind belong, and the other will be the class of things with an attribute – sometimes called the *differentia* – which distinguishes the thing in question from other members of the genus. For example, Aristotle defined man as a rational animal. Saving ourselves from the word *man*, we can say that human beings are first of all identified as members of the larger class of animals – that's the genus – and then as rational, an attribute which Aristotle takes to differentiate us from other animals. Aristotle's definition is not the only possible one, of course.

It is important to recognise that things belong to many classes, and may be distinguished from other members of a class by many different attributes. A good definition, therefore, is one that not only picks out things of the kind in question, but makes reference to a genus and attribute that express something fundamental about things of that kind. Consider, for instance, Plato's definition of man as a featherless biped. Even if the genus and attribute of this definition were sufficient to pick us out from everything else, the definition is something of a joke, if only because being featherless is hardly the fundamental attribute which distinguishes us from other bipeds.

Apart from failing to specify essential attributes, there are a number of other failures that can spoil a definition. One is that the definition may be *too wide*, because it includes things other than those to which the term refers. If we defined a lake as a large body of water surrounded by land, that would be too wide a definition because it would include an inland sea. Similarly, a definition can be *too narrow*, by failing to include things that should fall under it. An old social studies reader in my possession defines commercial farming as the growing of crops for sale. This definition is too narrow because it excludes dairy farmers, for instance, and other farmers who raise livestock for commercial consumption.

Another thing to avoid in definition is the use of negative terms. Plato's definition could be faulted on this account. It tells us what human beings are not – they are not feathered – when we want to know what they are. Although it is unusual for a thing to be defined by what it lacks, there are cases where this is appropriate: for instance, with explicitly negative terms like *unfair* or *meaningless*, and implicitly negative ones, such as *shallow* and *bachelor*.

A definition should not be circular. Most obviously, you invite circularity if you introduce into a definition the very notion that you are attempting to define. If I were to define *fairness* as *being just or fair in dealing with one's fellows*, that would be to move in something of a circle, because I have reintroduced the notion of being fair in the definition, when that was what I was trying to define. We strike the same problem at one remove if we define words directly in terms of each other. We might define a sibling as either a brother or sister, for example, but we could not go on to define a brother as a male sibling without introducing circularity of this kind. It would be better to define a brother as a male who has the same parents as another person. Dictionary definitions are sometimes circular in this way: *deformed* may be defined as *misshapen*, and *misshapen* as *deformed*. Trading synonyms produces the problem here.

Finally, in constructing a definition we need to watch for the use of vague or obscure expressions and avoid figurative language. In constructing a definition we aim to make the meaning of an expression clear, and so there is obviously no point in introducing terms which are less clear than the one being defined. Metaphor and analogy are also unsuitable for definition because figurative comparisons rest upon unstated respects in which things are somewhat alike, while definitions aim at literal identity.

Having thought about the features of a good definition, let us now turn to tools that children can use in the classroom to help them understand how terms may be defined.

DEFINE

We may use *DEFINE* to construct definitions as the need arises. First we choose a suitable genus, and then we look for essential attributes that restrict us to the thing we are trying to define. Finally, we check what we have done against the criteria for a good definition and make any necessary changes.

Rather than try to introduce terms like *genus* and *differentia* to children, we are going to work with a pair of overlapping circles to represent them. The genus circle can be called the GENERAL KIND circle, and the circle for differentiating properties can be called the SPECIAL FEATURES circle. The overlap between the two circles will then represent just the things we need for the definition. Here is the recommended layout, showing a simple example:

Define: Kitten

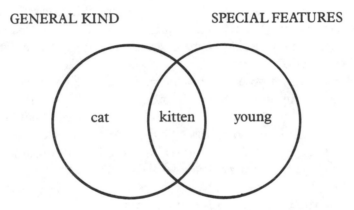

Definition: A kitten is a cat which is young.

Notice that in this example the definition first states the general kind and then adds a qualifying phrase for the special features. Rather than have children use such an awkward expression, you may prefer them to say simply that a kitten is a young cat, but I recommend the more cumbersome form of words, at least at the beginning, because it reflects the structure of genus plus distinguishing features. At the outset, you need to use every means available to encourage children to think in these terms. They can always tidy up the definition at the end.

Don't use *DEFINE* for individual work until the children show that they have a good understanding of the procedures. The sequence of steps set out below is somewhat artificial – as you'll see in the discussion of the example at the end of the section. So treat it as a guide rather than as a rigid prescription. Basically, the children need to co-ordinate two components in constructing a definition – the distinguishing features and the general kind – and this often involves changing their minds about one or the other as discussion proceeds.

Procedure

1. Having written down the term to be defined, turn to the GENERAL KIND circle. To what kind, more generally speaking, do things of this sort belong?

    There can be many answers to this question. Consider the term *mouse*. A mouse is a rodent, a vertebrate, an animal, a living thing and so on. Which should you choose? Here are two general rules to observe:

    (i)   Pick a kind that doesn't require you to produce a long list when you come to select special features. For instance, you could say that a mouse is a living thing, but then you would have to add *animal* to its list of distinguishing features.
    (ii) Choose a kind that suits your purposes. A librarian may wish to classify a dictionary as a reference holding, for instance, but in a primary classroom we might call a dictionary simply a book.

    Tentatively label the GENERAL KIND circle with your chosen kind.

2. Now turn to special features. You need to choose things essential to what you are trying to define that distinguish it from other things of that general kind. That will normally require some discussion. Supply these features in the SPECIAL FEATURES circle.

3. Now check your proposed definition against the following criteria:
    (i)   Is the definition too wide? In other words, can you think of anything that could be included in this definition that should not be there?
    (ii)   Is the definition too narrow? That is, can you think of an example that would be excluded by it, but which should not be excluded?
    (iii) Are the special features the essential ones?
    (iv)   Does the definition contain negative terms? Can you avoid them?
    (v)   Have you used any words that may not be clear?

Examples

1. Define: stalk

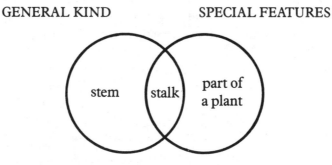

GENERAL KIND   SPECIAL FEATURES

stem   stalk   part of a plant

Definition: A stalk is a stem which is part of a plant. (*Tidy version:* A stalk is the stem of a plant.)

Some children will think that the general kind here is part of a plant, and that the distinguishing feature is that it's a stem. This has a different conceptual focus, as you can see:

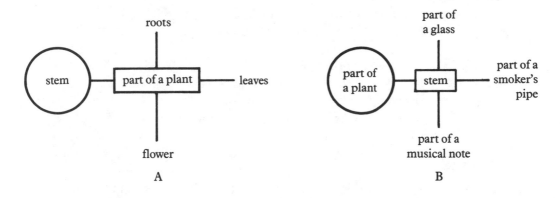

A

B

Neither way of thinking about the matter is wrong. Whether it is better to define a stalk as that part of a plant which is its stem, or as a stem that's part of a plant, depends upon the context. If our focus was on plants, we would probably choose the former (A) because the context specifies that we're dealing with plants. If we began by thinking about stems, however, we would probably prefer the latter (B). I raise this because it is important to note that the way we define things can depend upon our interests, and it is also a good conceptual exercise for children to see that things can be conceived from different points of view.

2. **Define: spoon**

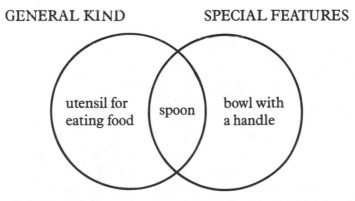

Definition: A spoon is a utensil for eating food which has a bowl with a handle.

A seasoned Year 6 class has gone through the basic steps to produce this definition, which is now on the board. Further discussion ensues:

Sandra: This definition is too narrow, because there are *mixing spoons* and they aren't used for eating.

Joseph: I can help with what Sandra said. We could say that a spoon is something you use for *handling* food.

Teacher: So which circle do you think we should change, Joseph?

Joseph: GENERAL KIND. We could change it to 'something for handling food'.

Robert: No, 'a *utensil* for handling food'.

Teacher: Is that alright with you, Joseph and Sandra? Okay. *(Changes the description on the board.)*

Bethan: The definition is too wide now. You use a saucepan for handling food, and it has a bowl with a handle. But it isn't a spoon!

Mira: Well, let's say that a spoon has a bowl with a handle, but it's not for cooking things in.

Teacher: Let's see. Mira, do you mean that we could take account of what Bethan said by adding 'not for cooking things in' to the other (SPECIAL FEATURES) circle?

Mira: Yes.

Robert: But Mira only said what a spoon is not. She said it's *not* for cooking things in.

Teacher: So it's *negative*. Thank you, Robert. But can you think of a different way of avoiding Bethan's problem? *(Pause)* Can someone else help out here?

Bernie: Why don't we change what Joseph said, and say that it's the kind of thing that you use for mixing or for eating food?

Robert: Utensil for mixing or eating food.

Bernie: We could put that in the circle.

Teacher: Which one do you mean, Bernie?

Bernie: Um, GENERAL KIND.

(The teacher changes GENERAL KIND to read 'utensil for mixing or eating food'.)

Isabel: I think that the definition is too narrow now. I was thinking about ladles. A ladle is a spoon – a special kind of spoon – but you don't eat with it or use it to mix food.

Joseph: A ladle isn't a spoon.

Isabel: Yes, it is. It's a spoon that you use to serve soup and things like that.

Teacher: What do other people think about what Isabel has said?

(Disagreement follows, while Robert looks up the word 'ladle' in the dictionary.)

Robert: It says here that a ladle is a large spoon.

Joseph: I don't agree with that!

As the discussion goes on, it appears that the concept of a spoon may be a bit fuzzy around the edges. Finally Robert introduces the word *conveying*, and after some discussion of what that means, the class finally agrees that the best definition is the following: 'A spoon is a utensil for mixing or conveying food and has a bowl with a handle.'

Classification

Classification provides another way of thinking about the genus and differentiating characteristics of definitions. When Aristotle defined humans as rational animals, he effectively divided animals into two classes – *animals with reason* and *animals without reason*:

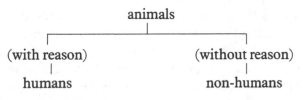

This is a simple example of what logicians call *dichotomous division* (cutting in two). We can use dichotomy to divide a genus in many different ways. For instance, we can divide animals into *animals with backbones* and *animals without backbones*, a division rather different from Aristotle's, which picks out the biological class of animals that we call *vertebrates*:

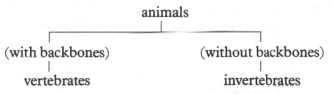

We can also apply the same process to each of our sub-divisions, and carry on down, each time calling upon a suitable distinguishing characteristic to further divide the genus. Alternatively, we can explore particular divisions, according to our interests, as in the following case, where we happen to be investigating native animals such as the platypus:

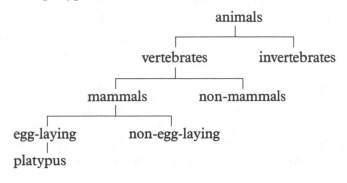

When carried out systematically, this is one way of producing a classification scheme. As we can see from the partly completed scheme above, some of its categories will turn out to be negative – invertebates, non-mammals, non-egg-laying – and it would probably not be useful for many purposes (including biology). All the same, it clearly illustrates the process of dividing larger classes into smaller ones by making successive distinctions – a process which underlies all classification schemes. Moving in the opposite direction, it also shows us how classification successively connects something with other things of an increasingly more general kind. For instance, by moving back up a pathway through the divisions in the sample above, we could classify mammals as vertebrate animals, or the platypus as an egg-laying, mammalian, vertebrate animal.

When working with classification, as with definition, always bear in mind that the distinctions and connections we make are relative to our purposes. For example, we usually divide schools into primary and secondary when we consider the stages of basic education, but we divide them into state, church and private when we think of them in terms of the educational provider. Similarly, while zoology might classify tigers as striped feline quadrupeds, environmentalists are more likely to list them under endangered species. These are different ways of classifying tigers according to our interests.

Classification can be a difficult and confusing task, even though it is fundamental to almost all human activity. So it is important to understand its basic principles. The tools provided here are designed to give children an elementary understanding of this kind of categorical thinking.

ARMS

ARMS is a tool for arranging a given collection of things into a dichotomous classificatory scheme. I recommend *ARMS* for small group activity.

Procedure

1. Divide the class into small groups. Ask each group to consider the collection of things in question and to ask: 'What do *all* these things have in common?' They should choose some common feature as the basic classification with which to begin.
2. Next they need to ask themselves what is the most significant feature, given their interests, which some things in the collection have, but others do not have. They can use this feature to make a first division into things which have that feature and things which lack it.
3. Now they should look for other significant features that might help them to divide these smaller groups, and make a further division.
4. They should keep on going in this way until they have made all the distinctions that seem appropriate to the collection.

Example

Classify: caves, burrows, cocoons, shells.

These are all things to be found in nature which can shelter living creatures. 'Things found in nature' would be a very broad class from which to begin, so let's take 'shelter for living creatures' as our starting point, and apply the procedures.

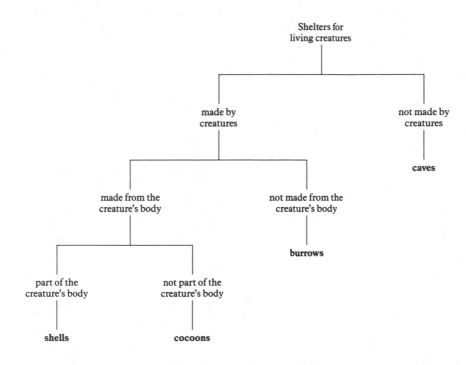

GROUP AND NON-GROUP

Here is a simpler version of dichotomous division for younger children. It stresses the fact that there are many possibilities for dividing up a group. It would be a good activity for children working in pairs, and could profitably be followed up with class discussion.

Procedure

1. Place a collection of objects on a tray, or begin in some other way with a specified collection of things.
2. Ask the children to see how many ways they can find to divide the collection into group and non-group categories. You need to specify that a group should consist of, say, at least three things from the collection. You might ask the children to make simple lists of their group categories if they are dealing with objects.

Example

The example below for lower primary shows one way of setting things out. The things in the group have been ticked, and the non-group things left blank. As in the example, it can be useful to suggest one division to start things off.

	HOME/NOT HOME		
feathers			
burrow	√		
grass			
coat			
bird			
house	√		
fur			
nest	√		
child			
seeds			
rabbit			

ANIMAL, VEGETABLE OR MINERAL?

An activity for younger children which has many of the same features as *ARMS* is the old game of *ANIMAL, VEGETABLE OR MINERAL?* One child gets to choose something that is either animal, vegetable or mineral – but doesn't tell what it is. Then go around the class, with each person asking that child a question, trying to determine what thing has been chosen. Only questions which ask whether the thing is of some particular kind are allowed. These would be questions like:

Is it animal?
Does it grow from seeds?
Is it something that you find in the ground?
Might it live in the zoo?
Is it a monkey?

The child who knows the answer simply answers either 'Yes', 'No' or 'Maybe', until someone manages to home in on the right answer. Anyone should be allowed to try to guess the answer at any stage, but it is useful to have a rule that each person is allowed only one guess.

TREE

TREE is a tool for constructing a general classification scheme for some specified genus. The genus might be animals, furniture, clothing, buildings, games, or whatever. Such schemes are more difficult to construct than the simple dichotomous division of a given collection. All the same, you will see that the rules which apply to dichotomous division also apply to general classification schemes. There are three principles to follow:

1. *Each division should appeal to only one characteristic.* If you try to divide a genus into groups without observing this rule, you are likely to end up with overlapping classes. As logicians would say, your classes will not be *mutually exclusive*. If I divided animals into those that live in the sea and those that breathe air, for instance, then I would have appealed to two characteristics (*sea-dwelling* and *air-breathing*) and would end up with overlapping classes. Whales, for example, would belong in both groups.

2. *Each division should include everything in the class being divided.* As logicians would say, the mutually exclusive categories of a division must also be *jointly exhaustive*, so that we omit nothing as we continue to divide. If I divided animals into sea-dwelling creatures and mammals, then that division would not be jointly exhaustive. Not all animals are either sea-dwelling or mammals. (The division wouldn't be mutually exclusive either, of course.)

3. *Each division should appeal to a characteristic of the same basic kind as the one with which we began.* For instance, if we began dividing animals according to their habitat, we should follow that basic principle all the way down through our divisions. Creatures that live in water, for example, might live in fresh water or in salt water, and creatures that live in salt water might live in shallow waters, on the sea bed and so on.

Procedure

1. *Break the general kind into two or more large groups.* The choice of groups is up to the children, but don't forget that there will usually be well-known ways in which other people have already classified the things in which the children are interested. If they are trying to classify things that we make (such as buildings, furniture or clothes), then it is usually a good idea for them to think about dividing those things according to their function – that is, the purposes for which they are used.

   In carrying out a division, we need to make sure that the resulting groups obey two rules, based on the principles described above:
   (i) *They should not leave anything out.* Everything of the general kind that we are dividing up into groups must belong to one of our groups.
   (ii) *They should not overlap.* Nothing of the general kind that we are dividing may belong to more than one group.

2. *Divide any of the groups into smaller groups as many times as is useful.* Whenever the children do so, however, they should be sure to use the same basis for division as before. For example, if they began by dividing things according to their shape, then they should go on dividing things according to their shape. If they began by dividing them according to their use, then they should go on dividing them according to their use, and so on.

Once again, the same two rules need to be observed: *try not to leave anything out and try to avoid any overlap between the groups.*

Example

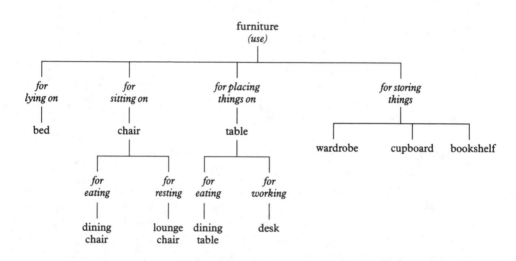

You will notice that in this attempt to classify furniture the categories are not actually exhaustive. Some kinds of furniture – such as sofas, stools and coffee tables – have been left out. Nor will all of the groups turn out to be mutually exclusive. A sofa might be used either for sitting on or for lying on, for example. As I said earlier, general classification schemes can be surprisingly difficult to construct. The educational benefit lies in the attempt, however, and even partial success deserves praise.

GROUP

GROUP is a simpler activity in which children attempt to produce classification schemes for themselves. It uses a mixture of work in pairs and class discussion.

Procedure

1. Begin with a group of things to be classified. You could present children with a group of actual objects, a list of things, or a group of pictures.

2. Divide the class into pairs, and have each pair discuss how to order the things into groups.
3. Afterwards have the class discuss any differences between the orderings produced.

There are a number of different ways of implementing this basic procedure. The example on the previous page, which uses pictures that can be cut out and arranged in groups, is designed for children in the beginning years of school.

Example

Divide the class into pairs and give each pair a copy of the pictures shown on page 85. Have each pair discuss how to group the animals depicted. They can cut out the pictures and work through their ideas before gluing them onto a sheet of paper.

Afterwards have the class discuss any differences between the groupings produced.

This completes our excursion into conceptual exploration, definition and classification. I have attempted to provide a variety of tools suitable for both older and younger children. These tools are generally adaptable, and lend themselves to small group activities once children are familiar with them. As your students begin to explore ideas, these conceptual tools will provide many opportunities to build upon class discussion.

NOTES
1. *TARGET* is adapted from Matthew Lipman & Ann Margaret Sharp, *Wondering at the World* (Lanham, Md.: University Press of America, 1986).
2. *CRAZY CASE* was suggested to me by John Wilson's discussion of what he calls 'contrary cases' in his book *Thinking with Concepts* (Cambridge: Cambridge University Press, 1963).
3. *BRIDGE* was suggested to me by an activity I observed in a philosophy class run by Beverly Peters at Northbridge Primary School in Sydney. Children from that class can be seen working on the activity in the accompanying photograph.
4. This example appears in a slightly different form in Philip Cam, *Thinking Stories 2: Teacher Resource/Activity Book* (Sydney: Hale & Iremonger, 1994), pp. 48-9.

CHAPTER SEVEN

Reasoning Tools

When we reflect upon some claim because we are uncertain of its implications or its truth, we ask ourselves questions such as: 'Does the claim *imply* things that we know to be untrue? Does it *assume* things that may be in conflict with the evidence? Does it fly in the face of what it is otherwise *reasonable* to assume? Can we think of *more plausible possibilities*?' Reflections of this kind involve us in reasoning.

Classroom inquiry, by its nature, focuses upon uncertain claims, looks at different possibilities and conjectures, and so invites us to reason. Since *reasoning is a connected sequence of thought that is directed toward a conclusion*, in discussion you will frequently hear children using forms of words such as:

- Since _____ then _____.

- We know that _____ and therefore _____.

- If _____ then _____.

Words such as these indicate that children are reasoning. You will also hear them making use of a range of little words that have special logical significance – words such as *some, all, no, not, and, but, unless, or,* and *only.* These are words that indicate the *logical form* of an utterance, as opposed to its particular content or subject matter. In this chapter we will deal with these kinds of words and constructions in looking at some ways of reasoning that will repay attention in the classroom.

Hypothetical Reasoning

When we inquire, we most often reason from what we believe to have happened, or from what we take to be true, toward what we are trying to establish. We argue that since such-and-such is the case, so-and-so must be (or is likely to be) the case too. In the conduct of inquiry, however, we also explore what *would* or *might be* the consequences of some mere possibility. This may be because we are trying to see whether that possibility is worth pursuing, or because we are looking for evidence that it has already been realised, or because we are interested in the general connections between it and other states of affairs. Whatever our aim, in such cases we can be said to reason *hypothetically*.

Hypothetical questions

The kind of questions that most obviously invite hypothetical reasoning are those which themselves are said to be hypothetical. As you'll be aware, people sometimes resist questions on the grounds that they are 'purely hypothetical'. Yet anyone who has seen a politician dodge a question on this ground knows that hypothetical questions can be of considerable importance. Here are some questions which call for hypothetical reasoning:

- If that were to happen, what consequences would there be?
- What would (or might) happen if we were to take this course of action?
- If that had happened, what would it have shown?

These sorts of questions are of such general significance that we should do all we can to encourage children to develop the habit of asking them.

Introducing hypothetical reasoning in the classroom

A very simple exercise in hypothetical reasoning is simply to have children say what would happen if such-and-such occurs. For example, you could ask young children to examine a picture or illustration where things are in danger of going wrong. You can ask what would happen if the man slips off the ladder . . . and then what would happen, and so on.[1] You can also have fun with the 'What if such-and-such happened?' type of question by asking children to make up quirky examples. For instance, what if a piece of toast turned into a piece of ghost? Or what if hard-boiled eggs turned into hard-boiled legs? The children could then try to carry on with what might follow.[2] These are good ways of introducing the topic of hypothetical reasoning.

Planning, predicting, explaining

I would now like to draw attention to a basic pattern of argument that includes hypothetical reasoning.[3] While at first glance it may look rather trivial, you will soon see that it is important in the context of inquiry. Here is some reasoning which has that pattern:

1. If I can find a way to convince Mrs Silver that I have made her tortoise grow, then I will gain her affections.
2. I can find a way to convince Mrs Silver that I have made her tortoise grow.

Therefore: I will gain her affections.

This is one way of looking at Mr Hoppy's reasoning in the early pages of Roald Dahl's story *Esio Trot*.[4] Mr Hoppy's reasoning is that of a man who is forming a plan. He has an outcome in mind (winning Mrs Silver's affections) and thinks about one or more means to that end – such as convincing Mrs Silver that he has helped her tortoise to grow. So far, the outcome of Mr Hoppy's reasoning is hypothetical in its form: '*If* so-and-so means are employed,' he reasons, '*then* such-and-such an end will be achieved.' But look at the whole of Mr Hoppy's reasoning again, and notice that it has a certain pattern:

Call this **A**

1. If I can find a way to convince Mrs Silver that I have made her tortoise grow, then I will gain her affections. ← Call this **B**
2. I can find a way to convince Mrs Silver that I have made her tortoise grow. ← Here's **A** again

Therefore: I will gain her affections. ← Here's **B** again

So Mr Hoppy's reasoning, taken as a whole, assumes the following form:

1. If A then B
2. A

Therefore: B

It is a connected sequence of reasoning in which a *hypothetical statement* (a statement of the form 'If A then B') is asserted on the first line, followed by what is called the statement's *antecedent* (the part that immediately follows the 'if') on the second line. Then the hypothetical statement's *consequent* (the part that follows 'then') has been deduced from these two statements.

This form of reasoning is extremely important, for all its simplicity. Aside from its role in predicting and planning – a little glimpse of which we have just seen – it is also of use in *explaining* events in many contexts. In fact it is very closely related to a basic form of scientific explanation that can easily be introduced in elementary science education. By making the connection, you can help children to appreciate the logic of scientific explanation, and draw attention to the explanatory role played by hypotheses in science.

An example will help to explain what I mean:

Teacher: Why did the very hungry caterpillar come to be such a big, fat caterpillar?

Adrian: It's because all he did was eat.

Susan: Yes, if you keep on eating all the time, then you grow to be big and fat.

Now here's the children's explanation again, this time in terms of the reasoning schema:

1. If you keep on eating all the time, then you grow to be big and fat.
2. The very hungry caterpillar kept on eating all the time.

Therefore: The very hungry caterpillar grew to be big and fat.

Notice that it is impossible for the conclusion to be false while (1) and (2) are true. If they are true, then it must also be true. The conclusion *follows from the premises* – or as logicians say, it can be *deduced* from them.

Now this is exactly the logic of explanation by reference to laws in science. Here's an example, involving Newton's second law of motion, for comparison. Don't be concerned if you don't know the equation or units of measurement. Just notice that it begins with a general hypothetical statement (Newton's second law) followed by the statement of a condition that corresponds to its antecedent, from which a statement corresponding to the consequent has been deduced:

1. If a force F is applied to an object of mass m, then that object will accelerate according to $F = ma$, where a stands for acceleration. (Newton's second law)
2. A force of 50 newtons was applied to an object of mass 10kg.

Therefore: The object accelerated at 5 m/s^2.

The form of reasoning is just the same as in the case of the very hungry caterpillar. In the children's case, the hypothetical premise 'If you keep on eating all the time, then you'll grow big and fat' may not be exactly a scientific law, but it is a good step in that direction for someone of Susan's age. And together with Adrian's observation, Susan's 'law' explains the event that the children were asked to account for in exactly the same way that scientific laws help to explain events. So if you can engage children in this form of reasoning, and bring them to reflect upon its logic, you will have accomplished something of importance in developing their ability to think scientifically.

The need to be explicit

Let me insert a note here about the need for generalisations to be made explicit. When children are trying to explain events, to justify behaviour, or to judge the worth of something, they will most likely not mention the general hypotheses that underpin what they say. We all do that, of course. If you were to ask me why the plant in my office is nearly dead, and I were to say that it's because I forgot to water it, it would be needless for me to add that *if a plant lacks water, then eventually it will die*. I can rely upon you to know that elementary fact and to use it in following my explanation. When we venture into more problematic or less familiar territory, however, these underlying claims more often need to be made explicit and subjected to scrutiny.

Making our guiding hypotheses explicit is normal practice in philosophical inquiry. We subject our hypotheses to reason, just as in science we test them experimentally. Consider this example:

> *Karen:* Mrs Silver didn't have to do anything for Mr Hoppy if she didn't want to.
> *Justin:* Yes, she did.
> *Jesse:* Why, Justin?
> *Justin:* Because he helped her by making her tortoise grow.
> *Jesse:* So?
> *Justin:* So she owed him something. Right?
> *Karen:* Justin, you don't have to do something for someone else just because they do something for you.
> *Justin:* Look Karen! *If someone does something for you, then you have to do something for them.*

At last Justin has explicitly stated the principle of reciprocity that he has in mind. At this point the teacher could draw attention to the principle and encourage all the children to consider it. They might be asked to provide examples to illustrate their views, or to give other kinds of reasons for what they say. Things do not always go so smoothly, of course. Children who lack experience of philosophical inquiry will often rely upon a contentious principle like Justin's without ever making it explicit. In that case the teacher needs to coax it out into the open.

Testing hypothetical statements

This brings us to the important topic of testing hypothetical claims. Once again there are connections with scientific reasoning, and on that ground alone it is worth our attention. In experimental work, we subject our hypotheses to test by controlling their initial or antecedent conditions (those in the 'if' part), and then we look to see whether the predicted consequences ensue (in accordance with the 'then' part). If they don't come about, the hypothesis was wrong (unless we didn't properly control the initial conditions).

There is a direct connection between the logic of explanation and the logic of prediction that lies behind testing. Earlier we saw an example of prediction in the case of Mr Hoppy's reasoning, but for something more akin to science let's look again at Adrian and Susan's explanation of how the very hungry caterpillar grew to be big and fat:

1.   If you keep on eating all the time, then you grow to be big and fat.
2.   The very hungry caterpillar kept on eating all the time.

Therefore: The very hungry caterpillar grew to be big and fat.

Suppose that instead of explaining how the caterpillar grew to be big and fat, Susan and Adrian had looked only at the first part of the story and were predicting that it would grow to be big and fat. They would use just the same form of reasoning, only this time they would be relying upon the generalisation and their observation of the caterpillar's behaviour to predict the outcome:

1.   If you keep on eating all the time, then you grow to be big and fat.
2.   The very hungry caterpillar keeps on eating all the time.

Therefore: The very hungry caterpillar will grow big and fat.

Because prediction is an essential part of testing, becoming familiar with this form of reasoning is learning an important part of the logic of testing. In this case, the children's prediction would be borne out by what happens in the rest of the story, and so Susan's hypothesis would survive the 'test'. In science, of course, the test would probably be experimental. Even so, learning to think in this way is an *essential* part of learning to think scientifically, and should be addressed in the early years of school.

In philosophical inquiry we can also put our guiding hypotheses to the test. A common form of test is the search for examples which run counter to the hypothesis. We look for a case (either real or imaginary) which satisfies the antecedent but violates the consequent. If the hypothesis is true, there will be no such examples. So if we find one, then the hypothesis isn't true! Such examples are called *counter-examples* and play an analogous role in philosophical inquiry to disconfirming evidence in scientific inquiry. Although the example is really scientific rather than philosophical, Adrian might offer a counter-example to Susan's hypothesis – that if you keep on eating all the time, then you will grow big and fat – by saying that he has a sister who is a champion swimmer, and she eats all the time but isn't big and fat. (By the way, I wonder what Adrian means by '*all* the time'?) On the philosophical side, taking Justin's hypothesis – that if someone does something for you, then you have to do something for them – a counter-example *might* be a priest who hears a man's confession. The priest does something for the man. But is the man thereby obligated to do something for that priest? If not, then Justin's principle can't be true, without qualification.

Testing the antecedent

We can also use hypothetical statements to test whether their antecedents (or 'if' parts) are true. Consider the reasoning employed by the scornful princess in the following snippet of conversation:

Princess: You're not a prince. You're just an ugly old toad.

Toad: But I am a prince, I tell you.

Princess: If you're a prince, then I'm . . . a roast duck!

The toad *is* a prince, of course, and that makes the princess's last remark rather unwise. The point of her remark, however, is to assert the absurdity of the toad's claim to be a prince, and the logic behind the remark runs as follows:

1. If you're a prince, then I'm a roast duck.
2. (Obviously) I'm not a roast duck.

Therefore: You're not a prince.

Once again we can strip away the subject matter of this piece of reasoning to reveal its form, and we will end up with something like this:

1. If *A* then *B*.
2. It's not the case that *B*.

Therefore: It's not the case that *A*.

Here hypothetical reasoning is used to deny the antecedent. The reasoning is that (hypothetically) if *so-and-so* were the case, then *such-and-such* ought to be the case; but *such-and-such* turns out not to be the case, and therefore neither does *so-and-so*.

The problem with the princess's argument is that, while her reasoning is fine, her second premise is not as reliable as she takes it to be. The moral is that we need to be certain of the reliability of our premises before we can safely use them to infer the truth of our conclusion.

This ends our brief tour of the elementary logic of planning, prediction, explanation, and testing hypotheses. These are large topics, but I hope that enough has been said to draw attention to them and to indicate something of their importance. While much of this logic is rooted in everyday exploratory behaviour, a reflective understanding of its processes is not automatic. So they are topics that demand attention as children learn to make their way in inquiry in many aspects of their learning.

Inductive Reasoning

There is something important that the following three remarks have in common:

George: There are three Vietnamese kids in my class. None of them can speak English properly. I'll bet there isn't a Vietnamese kid in the school who can speak English.

Patricia: At lunchtime I saw Miss Cooper going out of the school gate in a car with Mr Wilson. I think they must be in love with each other.

Leslie: We have a fat kid in out class. Boy, is he lazy! Isn't that typical.

It seems that George is prejudiced against the Vietnamese children in his school. Patricia thinks that if a man and a woman go off in a car together, it means that they're 'in love'. Leslie is using a stereotype to brand a classmate. So what do these things have in common? One thing is that they all involve unwarranted generalisation.

We are sometimes told not to generalise. Presumably this means that we should not generalise *without respecting the differences that exist*. For we generalise whenever we learn from experience, and nobody would tell us that we shouldn't learn from experience. Without generalisation we wouldn't believe that the sun will rise tomorrow, or that the next child who enters the classroom will not have two heads. It is vital (and to some extent inevitable) that we should generalise. Instead of avoiding generalisation, we need to avoid conclusions based on un-reliable samples; we need to be open to contrary evidence; and we need to consider whether the connections we make are plausible in the light of other things that we know.

We can also be more or less dogmatic in the way that we hold to our generalis-ations. The more dogmatic we are, the less we are likely to be receptive to evidence that doesn't fit, and the less we are likely to think about whether our cherished views are consistent with, or borne out by, the many things that we have had the chance to observe or in some other way come to know. So whether we function well with generalisation or not is partly a matter of attitude. Being prepared to look at the evidence – for and against – and to regard a generalisation more as a *working hypothesis* than an indubitable truth is an important part of being intelligent in the way that we uphold our views.

It is best to attend to these matters in the early years, when the chances of developing good habits are strong. One part of a sound educational strategy, recommended here, is to give children the opportunity to engage in inductive reasoning together on topics that relate to their concerns and experience. Through reasoning with one another, they can learn to generalise in a considered and principled way.

The logical form of generalisations

The three basic categories of generalisation are *always, never* and *generally*. When people make generalisations, sometimes they don't make it entirely clear whether their claim is meant to be universal – so that it applies to *everything* in the nomi-nated class – or whether it *usually* or *generally* applies. While someone who says that politicians are dishonest probably means that they are *generally* dishonest, tend to be dishonest, or are more dishonest than most other groups of people, they might mean *all*. Likewise, someone who says that men are misogynists might mean that *all* men are misogynists, or that they are *generally* misogynists, or that a large proportion of men have tendencies in that direction. So the first thing we often need to do in considering a generalisation is to clarify the force of the claim being made. Does the person mean *all* or *always*, or do they mean nearly always, generally, or that there is a tendency of some kind to be observed?

Universal generalisations are ones of the strictly 'all' or 'none' kind, and their standard logical form is either 'All *A* are *B*' or 'No *A* is *B*'. Here are some examples to which the standard logical form has been added in italics:

Children with messy desks always have untidy handwriting.

All children with messy desks are children with untidy handwriting.

Anyone who wants more ice-cream is a greedy pig.

All those people who want more ice-cream are greedy pigs.

Lions are carnivores.

All lions are carnivores.

None of the boys in Mr Brunton's class have done their homework.

No boy in Mr Brunton's class is someone who has done his homework.

There is no one in the class who knows the answer.

No member of the class is someone who knows the answer.

Blowflies are not beautiful.
No blowfly is beautiful.

As we saw in the previous section, sentences of the form 'If _____ then _____' are also a common way of framing a generalisation. It is worth noting, therefore, that a statement of this form can be translated into one of the form 'All _____ are _____'. For instance, in the examples above we might just as easily have said, 'If children have untidy desks, then they will have untidy handwriting' or 'If anyone wants more ice-cream, then he or she is a greedy pig'. These statements make the same claim as their non-hypothetical partners, and can be translated into the same standard 'All _____ are _____' form.

While for most purposes it is not necessary to translate generalisations into their standard form, knowing the standard form helps us to see the logical character of the claim being made. We can also use a pair of overlapping circles to make the logic of our generalisations explicit. We can simply let each circle represent one of the classes of things in question, with the overlap representing things (if there are any) which fall into both classes. The part of the *A* circle that lies outside the *B* circle represents those *A*s which are not *B*s, while the part of the *B* circle that lies outside of the *A* circle represents those *B*s which are not *A*s. We can indicate that there is no *A* which is *B*, no *A* which is *not B*, or no *B* which is *not A*, by shading in the area that, according to our statement, has nothing in it. In the case of a statement of the form 'No A is B' we would shade the overlap between the circles to indicate that there is nothing which is both *A* and *B*:

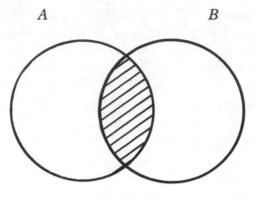

'No *A* is *B*'

For a statement of the form 'All *A* are *B*' this would result in the following:

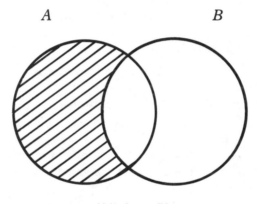

'All *A* are *B*'

That is to say, the part of the *A* circle which lies outside of the *B* circle has no *A*s in it – because anything which is *A* is also *B*.

This procedure also helps to make clear what is required in a counter-example to a generalisation of either kind. There will be one or more counter-examples if the shaded segment is not really as indicated. A counter-example to an 'all' statement would be an example which involves an A which is not a *B* (or a *B* which is not an *A* in the case of 'All *B* are *A*'), just as a counter-example to a 'no' statement would involve an *A* which is also a *B*.

Some criteria for evaluating generalisations

On occasions when a generalisation is questionable and it becomes appropriate to ask whether it can be sustained, there are a number of things that need to be considered. The following three questions may serve as a rough guide in the classroom:

1. Is the claim based upon adequate evidence?

At six years of age, Patricia believes that all Year 1 teachers are women. It isn't clear whether Patricia's claim is meant to apply to all Year 1 teachers no matter where they teach; but let's say, rather vaguely, that it is supposed to apply just to current Year 1 teachers in schools round about. Patricia's main piece of evidence, in any event, is that all the Year 1 teachers she has ever known are women. Yet since the only Year 1 teachers that Patricia has known are the three who teach in her school, her evidence for this generalisation is hardly adequate. Patricia's sample of Year 1 teachers is too small.

What would constitute an *adequate sample* in such a case? Perhaps nothing short of a complete enumeration of every Year 1 teacher in the schools round about would suffice to determine the matter. Yet while we may find such a count feasible on this occasion, obviously there are cases where an exhaustive inquiry is out of the question; and, like those who conduct surveys, we will have to rely upon samples.

Patricia's problem may be just one of sample size, but in many cases we also have to be concerned about whether the evidence we muster is *representative*. Leslie believes that all fat people are lazy. Although this is probably a view that Leslie has acquired from others and the media, when pressed for evidence Leslie can cite the boy in his class, and maybe one or two other examples. There may be a lazy fat person in his favourite television show and his Uncle Joe, who has a reputation in the family for being lazy. The question is how representative this evidence is of overweight people in general. It would serve Leslie's case better if a wider range of evidence was brought to bear.

2. Has there been a search for counter-examples?

Aside from considering the evidence in favour of a generalisation, we need to look for evidence that might show it to be mistaken. With a little reflection, sometimes this is surprisingly easy to come by. Patricia has the idea that if two people (or at any rate, two *teachers*), such as Mr Wilson and Miss Cooper, go off together in a car on some occasion such as in the lunch hour, then they are 'in love'. The fact that there may be no further supporting evidence in this case, and quite a lot of disconfirming evidence in general, may well be known to Patricia if only she were to consider the matter.

In looking for counter-examples or contrary evidence, it is often a good idea to consider marginal or atypical cases. Do all birds fly? Well, have we considered penguins? Is the time that elapses between one sunrise and the next always about 24 hours? Well, what should we say about regions near the poles? By sticking with typical or paradigm cases – the kind that come most easily to mind – we may be confirming a generalisation which does not always apply.

3. Can we explain the connection?

When Tim and Leonie return from a holiday without their dog, they get bitten by fleas. They have never been bitten by fleas before and they suppose that maybe the fleas are biting because they're angry about being left alone. When the children are told that fleas bite just because they're fleas, they don't find that explanation very satisfactory. 'Dogs don't bite,' says Leonie, 'unless they have been badly treated.' 'So why would something bite just because it's a flea?' asks Tim.

Frankly, the children are a little sceptical of the general proposition that all fleas bite, and given their limited knowledge of fleas, that's fair enough. They soon change their minds, however, when they find out that a flea bite is not like a dog bite, and that fleas are blood-sucking insects which live off the blood of the animals they bite. This piece of information makes the claim that *if it's a flea, then it bites* more compelling than any number of flea bites ever would. It takes us beyond the cases that count as evidence for or against that claim to an explanation of the link between being a flea and biting which guarantees that all fleas bite.

As we have just seen, other things we know or can find out may make a generalisation more plausible – or *less* plausible – and may provide an explanation of why that general connection should hold. It may turn out that a generalisation is based more upon our presuppositions than on evidence, of course, and these presuppositions can all too readily help to confirm whatever evidence we tend to see. Such is the nature of bias and prejudice. Yet once we begin to examine these presuppositions in the light of day, we may see them for the poorly founded assumptions that they are, and then the generalisations that they nourish will themselves begin to wither.

Analogical Reasoning

In analogy we draw attention to a similarity or resemblance between things that are different in other respects. By making these connections we integrate experience and enlarge upon its meaning. If the farmer's unshaven chin is described as being *rough as stubble in the field*, we connect the farmer with his harvested land through the appearance and feel of his chin. If we say that the boy recoiled from his mother's boiled cabbage *like the mother from his dirty socks*, we capture the boy's repulsion by the counterpoise of the mother's disgust. If we picture a ship at sea in the night, sailing through waves *like the moon through clouds*, we tie the elements of the scene together, creating a mood.

Like analogy, metaphor is also an invaluable means of linguistic invention. We can say that stubble covered the farmer's chin, or that the ship's sail was a crescent moon gliding through the clouds. Here we have exchanged the comparison of analogy for the identity of metaphor. Metaphor is also a means of suggesting possibilities and fresh understandings in many fields of inquiry. It is commonly said that William Harvey discovered the heart to be a pump, for instance, although that description is really a metaphorical way of expressing the new understanding that his discoveries produced. Some years ago, the English zoologist Desmond Morris described humans as naked apes in order to nudge us into a new orientation towards our species. More extended metaphors can provide a profusion of possibilities to guide inquiry. The wave of research based on the idea of the mind as a computer would be a good example.

Obviously we should encourage children to be aware of figurative language, and to learn how to make effective use of it. Don't forget that they are already accustomed to thinking in such terms, although they may not have reflected upon it. Name-calling, for instance, is a vivid use of metaphor. Riddles often begin with metaphor or invite analogical thinking. Consider 'What has three eyes and one leg?' or 'Why is an island like the letter t?'[5] You can make use of such things in order to call attention to metaphorical and analogical thinking.

In the rest of this section I want to look particularly at the use of analogical reasoning in argument. To see the kind of thing I have in mind, suppose that someone were to argue as follows: *Thinking is like gardening. Just as a gardener needs gardening tools in order to garden well, a thinker needs thinking tools in order to think well. So you can't think well without thinking tools.* That would be an argument from analogy. It is an argument from a supposedly parallel or similar case, to the effect that what applies to that parallel case also applies to the case in question.

If it is to carry conviction, the analogous case must suggest the link that we want to press in the conclusion in a more obvious or compelling way. Thus the claim that a gardener needs gardening tools in order to garden well is supposed to exhibit clearly the kind of connection that is claimed to exist between thinking and thinking tools. This means that the argument works by relying upon *an unstated general claim, connection, or principle that both cases are supposed to exemplify.* The parallel case is merely a more obvious or familiar illustration. Since arguments from analogy seldom make the principle explicit, its precise formulation usually needs discussion or reflection. In our example, it might be something like *effective work demands that we employ appropriate tools.* In essence, the argument is that you can see this quite readily in the case of gardening; and once you see that tools are always required for effective work, you can see that it must apply to thinking too, because thinking is a kind of work.

The point that I am leading to is that arguments from analogy turn upon a *generalisation.* There is an implicit 'all' or 'no' statement involved. This is the fundamental (though hidden) feature of arguments from analogy, and the thing that we should always search for in them. When it comes to evaluating such arguments, we should not be swept away by an attractive analogy without asking ourselves what the analogy has in common with the case in question, and then trying to formulate an appropriate generalisation. For it is only through some general claim or principle which they both illustrate that the analogy supplies genuine support for the conclusion.

What I have just been saying might be merely of academic interest if arguments from analogy weren't so common and often so very persuasive. Just think of how frequently we try to persuade others (or indeed ourselves) not to take some course of action because we are struck by the similarity of the circumstances to other occasions on which that course of action proved unwise. Think also of the line of argument implicit in a great deal of advertising: *This person (or those people) are much like (or in similar circumstances to) you. Look at what such-and-such a product has done for them! Therefore it can do the same for you.* I am not saying that arguments from analogy are always bad, but merely that we need to view them critically. That means coming to understand how they work, and being able to discern the general claim upon which the legitimate force of the analogy rests.

That ends our discussion of reasoning tools. I hope that sufficient has been said to show the importance of paying attention to reasoning in the classroom. By learning to pay attention to their reasoning, and discovering its use in such processes as planning, predicting, explaining, generalising and reasoning with analogy, children will have acquired something of value not only for the classroom. When combined with the facility that children can develop with concepts, it will provide them with tools of lasting value in everyday life.

Conclusion

Thinking Together explores the use of philosophy to promote good thinking in the primary classroom. It shows how philosophical inquiry can be viewed as an educational activity in which children raise questions and investigate issues using the tools and procedures of philosophy. We have seen how the philosophical riches and intellectual adventure of children's literature can be a springboard for inquiry, and I have indicated how to plan class discussion and other activities around story materials, and discussed many things that the teacher needs to do in building a community of inquiry.

I hope that *Thinking Together* will prove a useful introduction for the teacher, but the most valuable aid to learning about philosophical inquiry with children is doing it in the classroom.

NOTES

1. For example see the picture 'What Happens Next?' in Michael Rosen and Quentin Blake, *Hard-Boiled Legs* (London: Walker Books, 1987).
2. The examples come from *Hard-Boiled Legs*.
3. Aside from planning, predicting and explaining, this pattern of reasoning is also important for *testing hypotheses*. That's not surprising, of course, since testing involves prediction. I will deal with testing later in the chapter.
4. Roald Dahl, *Esio Trot* (Harmondsworth: Puffin Books, 1991).
5. See June Factor, *Ladles and Jellyspoons: Favourite Riddles and Jokes of Australian Children* (Ringwood, Victoria: Puffin Books, 1989). The first riddle is based on metaphor, while the second is obviously analogical. The answer to the first riddle, in case you haven't guessed it, is a traffic light. The answer given to the second riddle is because it's always in the middle of water!

Appendix: A Guide to Assessment

The following record sheet is designed to help the teacher make a qualitative judgement about the cognitive and interpersonal outcomes of the kind of classroom activity discussed in this book. It is meant to be applied to the class as a whole.

I have tried to keep the list short enough to be of practical use to a busy classroom teacher, but sufficently comprehensive and well balanced to give a fair indication of progress. I recommend an initial evaluation of the class's cognitive and social behaviour very soon after you have begun a program of inquiry, and then a second evaluation after at least a term of uninterrupted work. You might like to make a photocopy of these pages for that purpose.

I have also supplied some brief explanatory notes to help make each question on the list clear and definite.

---

	very seldom	some-times	quite often	almost always

A: Inquiry Skills

1. Do the children ask fruitful questions?
2. Do they consider reasons/evidence?
3. Do they seek explanations?
4. Do they explore alternatives?
5. Do they engage in self-correction?
6. Do they stick to the point?

B: Reasoning and Conceptual Skills

1. Do the children clarify meanings?
2. Do they make useful distinctions?
3. Do they make appropriate comparisons?
4. Do they give helpful examples?

	very seldom	some- times	quite often	almost always

5. Do they draw relevant inferences?
6. Do they make considered judgements?

C: Interaction Patterns

1. Do the children listen to each other?
2. Do they share the discussion?
3. Do they help each other?
4. Do they explore disagreements?
5. Do they show respect for each other's views?
6. Do they accept fair criticism of their ideas?

Notes

A.   Inquiry Skills

1. *Do the children ask fruitful questions?* Do they ask questions that draw attention to important concepts and significant issues? Do their questions lead to good discussion?
2. *Do they consider reasons/evidence?* Do the children offer reasons for their views and seek reasons for what other children say, when it is appropriate to do so? Do they try to evaluate the reasons that are offered? Do they think about what grounds or evidence would support contentious claims, or what would count against them?
3. *Do they seek explanations?* Do the children generally try to find reasons for things, and to explain what could cause something to happen?
4. *Do they explore alternatives?* Do the children tend to stick with one idea, or do they look for different possible explanations, different possible outcomes, and different ways of understanding something?
5. *Do they engage in self-correction?* Do the children revise positions that they recognise to be defective? Do they try to improve on their first thoughts? Do they sometimes say that they have changed their minds?
6. *Do they stick to the point?* How often do the children lose sight of the point being discussed, or change the topic without realising it? Does the discussion have sufficient focus, and proceed in an orderly way?

B. Reasoning and Conceptual Skills

1. *Do the children clarify meanings?* How often do the children discuss questions, statements or concepts that need clarification? Do they display skill in doing so?

2. *Do they make useful distinctions?* Do the children distinguish between things that are similar yet different in some important respect? Do they tend to make unwarranted generalisations?

3. *Do they make appropriate comparisons?* Do the children tend to make appropriate connections between things that they are discussing?

4. *Do they give helpful examples?* Do the children illustrate or explain what they say with examples when that would be helpful? Do they sometimes also use examples to try to show that some claim might not be correct?

5. *Do they draw relevant inferences?* Are the children alert to the consequences of their views? Do they tend to uncover questionable assumptions that have been made?

6. *Do they make considered judgements?* Do the children tend to leap to conclusions? Or do they weigh the evidence and take the relevant circumstances into account in coming to a judgement?

C: Interaction Patterns

1. *Do the children listen to each other?* Do they pay careful attention to what other children are saying and not just to the teacher? Are they listening *actively*?

2. *Do they share the discussion?* Is the class as a whole able to share in the discussion, or do a few people tend to dominate it? Are there people who sometimes get excluded from discussion? Do some people talk over the top of others, or cut other people off?

3. *Do they help each other?* Do the children tend to build on one another's ideas? Do they help someone who has difficulty in expressing what he or she wants to say? Do they co-operate well in small groups?

4. *Do they explore disagreements?* Do the children try to work out the basis of their disagreements? Do they try to investigate whether that basis is genuine? Do they explore the reasons they each have for their views, and whether there is room for a change of mind?

5. *Do they show respect for each other's views?* Are the children able to disagree, or express a different view, while restricting their criticism to ideas? Are they fair in the way they treat those with different opinions or preferences?

6. *Do they accept fair criticism of their ideas?* Do the children acknowledge that they may be wrong? Do they acknowledge that there may be another point of view? Do they sometimes agree with their critics against the ideas that they previously put forward?

Bibliography

References

Baron, Joan Boykoff & Sternberg, Robert J. (eds) 1987, *Teaching Thinking Skills: Theory and Practice*, W. H. Freeman, New York.

Ennis, Robert 1987, 'A taxonomy of critical thinking dispositions and abilities,' in Baron & Sternberg (eds), *Teaching Thinking Skills: Theory and Practice*.

Fisher, Robert 1991, *Teaching Children to Think*, Simon & Schuster Education, Hemel Hempstead.

Hullfish, H. Gordon & Smith, Philip 1967, *Reflective Thinking: The Method of Education*, Dodd, Mead & Company, New York.

Kelley, David 1988, *The Art of Reasoning*, W. W. Norton, New York.

Lakoff, George & Johnson, Mark 1980, *Metaphors We Live By*, Chicago University Press, Chicago.

Lipman, Matthew & Sharp, Ann Margaret (eds) 1978, *Growing Up with Philosophy*, Temple University Press, Philadelphia.

Lipman, Matthew, Sharp, Ann Margaret & Oscanyan, Frederick S. 1980, *Philosophy in the Classroom*, 2nd ed., Temple University Press, Philadelphia.

Lipman, Matthew 1988, *Philosophy Goes to School*, Temple University Press, Philadelphia.

—— 1991, *Thinking in Education*, Cambridge University Press, New York.

—— (ed.) 1993, *Thinking Children and Education*, Kendall/Hunt, Dubuque, Iowa.

Matthews, Gareth B. 1980, *Philosophy and the Young Child*, Harvard University Press, Cambridge, Mass.

—— 1984, *Dialogues with Children*, Harvard University Press, Cambridge, Mass.

—— 1993, 'Philosophy and children's literature,' in Lipman (ed.), *Thinking Children and Education*.

Mead, George Herbert 1934, *Mind, Self, and Society from the Standpoint of a Social Behaviourist*, Charles W. Morris (ed.), University of Chicago Press, Chicago.

Metzler, Bernard M. 1990, 'Mead's social psychology,' in John Pickering & Martin

Skinner (eds), *From Sentience to Symbols: Readings in Consciousness*, Harvester Wheatsheaf.

Passmore, John 1969, 4th ed., *Talking Things Over*, Melbourne University Press, Melbourne.

Pritchard, Michael S. 1985, *Philosophical Adventures with Children*, University Press of America, Lanham, Maryland.

Reck, A. (ed.) 1964, *Selected Writings of George Herbert Mead*, University of Chicago Press, Chicago.

Reed, Ronald F. 1983, *Talking with Children*, Arden Press, Denver, Colorado.

Ryle, G. 1972, 'Thinking and self-teaching,' *Rice University Studies*, Vol. 58, No. 3. Reprinted in Lipman (ed.), *Thinking Children and Education*.

Sharp, Ann Margaret & Reed, Ronald F. (eds) 1991, *Studies in Philosophy for Children: Harry Stottlemeier's Discovery*, Temple University Press, Philadelphia.

Siegler, Robert S. 1991, *Children's Thinking*, 2nd ed., Prentice Hall, Englewood Cliffs, N.J.

Splitter, Laurance J. & Sharp, Ann M. forthcoming 1995, *Teaching for Better Thinking: The Classroom Community of Inquiry*, Australian Council for Educational Research, Melbourne.

Stebbing, L. Susan 1939, *Thinking to Some Purpose*, Penguin, Harmondsworth.

—— 1952, *A Modern Elementary Logic*, 5th ed., Methuen, London.

Vygotsky, L. S. 1962, *Thought and Language*, M.I.T. Press, Cambridge, Mass.

—— 1978, *Mind in Society: The Development of Higher Psychological Processes*, Michael Cole, Vera John-Steiner, Sylvia Scribner & Ellen Souberman (eds), Harvard University Press, Cambridge, Mass.

Wertsch, James V. 1985, *Vygotsky and the Social Formation of Mind*, Harvard University Press, Cambridge, Mass.

Wilson, John 1971, *Thinking with Concepts*, Cambridge University Press, London.

Children's Books and Classroom Materials

Argent, Kerry 1988, *Friends*, Omnibus/Puffin, Ringwood, Victoria.

Burningham, John 1991, *Aldo*, Jonathan Cape, London.

Cam, Philip (ed.) 1993, *Thinking Stories 1: Philosophical Inquiry for Children*, Hale & Iremonger, Sydney.

—— 1993, *Thinking Stories 1: Teacher Resource/Activity Book*, Hale & Iremonger, Sydney.

—— (ed.) 1994, *Thinking Stories 2: Philosophical Inquiry for Children*, Hale & Iremonger, Sydney.

—— 1994, *Thinking Stories 2: Teacher Resource/Activity Book*, Hale & Iremonger, Sydney.

Carle, Eric 1973, *I See a Song*, Hamish Hamilton, London.

—— 1974, *The Very Hungry Caterpillar*, Puffin, Harmondsworth.

Carroll, Lewis 1993, *Alice's Adventures in Wonderland*, in *The Complete Stories of Lewis Carroll*, Magpie, London.

Cole, Babette 1986, *Princess Smartypants*, Hamilton, London.

Dahl, Roald 1991, *Esio Trot*, Puffin, Harmondsworth.

de Haan, Chris, MacColl, San and McCutcheon, Lucy forthcoming 1995, *Philosophy with Kids*, Longmans, Melbourne.

Dr. Seuss 1958, *The Cat in the Hat Comes Back*, Random House, New York.

Factor, June 1989, *Ladles and Jellyspoons: Favourite Riddles and Jokes of Australian Children*, Puffin Books, Ringwood, Victoria.

Hunt, Nan 1981, *Whistle Up the Chimney*, Collins, Sydney.

Lindsay, Norman 1957, *The Magic Pudding*, Penguin Books, Ringwood, Victoria.

Lipman, Matthew 1988, *Elfie*, Institute for the Advancement of Philosophy for Children, Montclair State College, New Jersey.

—— 1989, *Pixie*, Australian Council for Educational Research, Hawthorn, Victoria.

—— 1989, *Kio and Gus*, Australian Council for Educational Research, Hawthorn, Victoria.

—— 1992, *Harry Stottlemeier's Discovery*, adapted by Laurance Splitter, Australian Council for Educational Research, Hawthorn, Victoria.

Lipman, Matthew & Sharp, Ann Margaret 1982, *Looking for Meaning: Instruction Manual to Accompany Pixie*, IAPC/University Press of America, Lanham, Maryland.

Lipman, Matthew, Sharp, Ann Margaret & Oscanyan, Frederick S. (eds) 1984, *Philosophical Inquiry: An Instruction Manual to Accompany Harry Stottlemeier's Discovery*, 2nd ed., IAPC/University Press of America, Lanham, Maryland.

Lipman, Matthew & Sharp, Ann Margaret 1986, *Wondering at the World: Instruction Manual to Accompany Kio and Gus*, IAPC/University Press of America, Lanham, Maryland.

Lipman, Matthew & Gazzard, Ann 1988, *Getting Our Thoughts Together: Instruction Manual to Accompany Elfie*, IAPC, Montclair State College, New Jersey.

Marks, Alan 1988, *Nowhere to be Found*, Picture Book Studio, Saxonville, Maryland.

Milne, A. A. 1928, *The House at Pooh Corner*, Methuen, London.

Murris, Karen 1992, *Teaching Philosophy with Picture Books*, Infonet Publications, London.

Rosen, Michael and Blake, Quentin 1987, *Hard-Boiled Legs*, Walker Books, London.

Ross, Tony 1987, *Foxy Fables*, Puffin, London.

Rowe, Don and Newton, Jan 1994, *You, Me, Us! Social and Moral Responsibility for Primary Schools*, Citizenship Foundation, London.

Sprod, Tim 1993, *Books into Ideas*, Hawker Brownlow Education, Melbourne.

Williams, A. E. & Eakins, C. 1980, *New Social Studies through Activities*, Martin Education, Sydney.